NO LAW,

MIKE GOLDING was born in 1960 and began sailing in the gravel pits around London, later weekend cruising with his parents on the south coast. At Reading Blue Coat School he was already achieving success in Solo class dinghies. A course at Lowestoft Nautical College included a period of commercial training aboard North Sea trawlers working in Icelandic waters. At seventeen he joined multihull designer Pat Patterson for the 'In the Wake of Drake' circumnavigation on which he learned a great deal about traditional navigation and seamanship.

In 1980 he joined the Royal Berkshire Fire and Rescue Service, later becoming a founding member of the National Fire Service Sailing Association. His yacht-racing career began with class wins in the Azores Race, competing in the Single-handed Transatlantic Race and the Round Britain and Ireland Race.

In 1991 he began his successful association with the yacht *Group 4* and the company which sponsored it when he was selected as one of the ten skippers for Chay Blyth's British Steel Challenge and led *Group 4* to first place on two of the four legs, being beaten overall by just seventy minutes. He is now the General Manager of Group 4 Securitas's training company, PromOcean, which specialises in team building and leadership skills.

No Law, No God

The fastest solo circumnavigation against winds and currents

Mike Golding

CORONET BOOKS
Hodder and Stoughton

Golding, Mike
    No Law, No God: Fastest Solo
    Circumnavigation Against Winds and
    Currents
    I. Title
    910.41

ISBN 0 340 64703 5

Printed and bound in Great Britain by
Cox & Wyman Ltd, Reading, Berkshire

Hodder and Stoughton
A division of Hodder Headline PLC
338 Euston Road
London NW1 3BH

For Chay, an inspiration to us all,
and for Philip for making it possible.

CONTENTS

Foreword by Chay Blyth   9
Introduction by Jørgen Philip-Sørensen   25

1 A Hidden Agenda   29

2 One Day at a Time
  (Day 1 – Day 17)   41

3 Driving Hard
  (Day 18 – Day 34)   51

4 Turn Right at the Horn
  (Day 35 – Day 45)   65

5 No Law, No God
  (Day 46 – Day 54)   77

6 The Longest Beat
  (Day 55 – Day 72)   89

7 Tasman Rendezvous
  (Day 73 – Day 84)   103

8 Gone West
  (Day 85 – Day 99)   117

9 The Ocean I Love to Hate
  (Day 100 – Day 121)   133

10 Knock Down
   (Day 122 – Day 139)   147

11 Stop-Go to Southampton
   (Day 140 – Day 167)   159

12 The Pinnacle   171

Appendix One:
The Challenge Fleet 67-foot One-Design Yacht Specification 177

Appendix Two:
The Group 4 Global Challenge Technical Specification   179

Appendix Three:
Food   183

Appendix Four:
Medical Supplies by Dr Campbell Mackenzie   187

FOREWORD
by CHAY BLYTH

When Mike approached me to say he would like to sail around the world in the hope of beating my time, and did I object, I was flattered that he should even consider it necessary to make such a request. The flattery increased when he asked me to write the foreword to this book chronicling his voyage.

There was never any doubt of my fullest support and backing for Mike. Equally, there was never any doubt in my mind that he would succeed. What none of us knew when he set off on his voyage was how well he would succeed.

I have never seen my circumnavigation in the yacht *British Steel* as a record. In 1970 no one had sailed non-stop around the world against the prevailing winds and currents. Yachting pundits and some very senior people advised me not to go. To me it was the ultimate adventure to be the first to achieve something. Sir Francis Chichester had sailed around the world some years before with only one stop, Robin Knox-Johnston followed him and had been the first man to sail around the world non-stop. Once a record has been set or a feat achieved, it is only a matter of time before someone does it faster, bigger, better. What would be the next step? I felt I was the man to sail around the world non-stop against the prevailing winds and currents.

Applying this rule, however, it was a surprise that no one else completed the same 'wrong way' circumnavigation non-stop and single-handed for twenty-two years. Maybe this shows how difficult that circumnavigation is. Even now I can close my eyes and see the legions of waves rushing towards me, one banked up against another.

Almost a quarter of a century ago the rule for severe-weather sailing when ploughing to windward was either to lie ahull (side on to the waves) or run before the wind. This tactic made it impossible to predict the length of a journey. Just how long would you be sitting in severe weather employing tactics whereby the yacht was either effectively in reverse or in neutral, drifting wherever she wanted?

The tactic I employed as the most reasonable to my mind was to lie ahull and drift, but all the time knowing that I was being pushed back by the howling winds and huge waves. I considered it worse still to run before the wind back in the direction I had just come with warps trailing to slow the yacht down. I managed not to succumb to that action! Using these tactics, how could anyone predict how long the circumnavigation was going to take? I took supplies for eighteen months!

Multihull sailing changed the theory about stopping progress during severe weather for one very basic reason. A multihull's least buoyancy is at its aft end. When they were lying ahull a wave could push the yacht back, sometimes flipping them over backwards. By continually sailing, even with a handkerchief for a sail, the yacht kept moving forward. It was infinitely safer than other options. The technique transferred to well-founded yachts who would power their way to windward. A major step forward had been established in tackling severe weather conditions and towards making the task of predicting passage times a finer art.

Mike's experience in multihulls means that he is well aware of this tactic and he had used it to great effect during the British Steel Challenge Round the World Yacht Race.

It came as no surprise to me, therefore, that Mike should sail around the world in a faster time than me. What was surprising was how much faster. This must be credited to his tenacity and his seamanship.

Some critical mention was made in the press that Mike's record could have been even faster had he not had to rendezvous to hand over logs and film for the PR machine of his sponsor. Sponsorship is not a modern phenomenon. Queen Isabella of Spain started sponsorship through her patronage of Christopher Columbus in the fifteenth century. She did not want publicity but the gold and land that new discoveries would bring. Artists, musicians, explorers and adventurers have always been dependent on others to provide them with the vehicle to achieve their individual success.

Thank God that today we have people like J. Philip-Sørensen,

Chairman of Group 4 Securitas. In many ways Philip was gambling on success as much as Mike. Thankfully, the gamble paid off for both of them and Mike's achievement brought back the goodies for his patron. Not land or gold but publicity – which in this day and age can have as great a value.

Mike's was a fantastic achievement that can never be taken from him. For me, I was delighted and honoured to stand shoulder to shoulder with both Mike and Philip and be a part of another great seafaring voyage.

CB
Cornwall, July 1994

ACKNOWLEDGMENTS

A huge team of people was responsible for the success of the Group 4 Global Challenge. It was their unselfish dedication during the preparation and whilst I was on passage that ensured a successful outcome.

My association with Group 4 companies around the world has provided me with three of the most challenging and eventful years of my life. The Chairman, Jørgen Philip-Sørensen, has been the most staunch supporter with the imagination and courage to support ventures which many others might have shied away from. The entire company actively supported both the British Steel Challenge crew and the Global Challenge but, in particular, I would like to thank Charles Rice who provided a constant link with the yacht throughout both the good and bad times. The control staff at Group 4's Headquarters provided the essential day to day contact with the yacht and Spencer Drummond, who provided the basis for the charts in this book, maintained a constant stream of objective support.

Chay's inspirational life has now touched many people's lives. His support for a project designed to better his time of twenty-two year before shows his unselfish willingness to offer others the chance to take up the challenges he has undertaken. I am grateful to Chay's company, The Challenge Business Ltd, who project managed the intense six-week preparation programme, headed by Andrew Roberts and his team – far too many to list.

Many companies, organisations and individuals diverted their time and resources far beyond those demanded by normal customers and I commend them for their high degree of dedication and professionalism in ensuring their products or services were more than equal to the task. I would like to extend my thanks to: Dr Campbell Mackenzie; Peter Vroon – Hood Sailmakers; Steve Moore – Autohelm/ Raytheon;

Henri Lloyd; Lewmar; David Freemantle – Proctor Masts; Maurice McQuitty – BT; all at BT's Portishead Radio; all at Bracknell Weather Centre (Metroute); the WSSRC; Royal Southampton Yacht Club; Royal Tasmanian Yacht Club, Hobart; Royal Cape Yacht Club, Cape Town.

Many of *Group 4's* crew from the Challenge Race lent their services and expertise to Global Challenge, in particular Mike O'Regan and Martin Hall who oversaw the preparations and worked long hours to make it all happen, and Donald Deakin and David Cowan who organised the food.

Last but by no means least Ceri and my family provided a wonderful source of inspiration and support – the kind that only real family and friends can offer.

Mike Golding

ILLUSTRATIONS

between pages 64 and 65

Trimming the headsail during Solent trials[1]
Adjusting the starboard autopilot control[1]
The autopilot[1]
Adjusting the leech line on the staysail[1]
Working on the deckplate aft of the mast
Trimming the staysail[1]
Plastic crates in lieu of crew
The single sideband radio[1]
A Christmas present form Chay[1]
Leaving Southampton[2]
Surfing past Gran Canaria
Good use of a poled out yankee[3]
In the doghouse bunk[1]
In the galley[1]
Turn right at Cape Horn
The full might of the Southern Ocean

between pages 160 and 161

Crashed out in the saloon between emergencies
Southern Ocean windward work
Rendezvous off Tasmania
A forty-foot roller sweeps the boat
Going well – in the wrong direction
Sailing westward at last
Off the Cape of Good Hope[4]
Rough weather in the South Atlantic

No Law, No God

Ideal trade wind sailing
The oily calm of the doldrums
A disorientated visitor
Dolphins were always welcome
Passing the Needles[1]
On the Shingles[1]
Waving to supporters[1]
Group 4 had sailed round the world[1]
The Global Challenge Trophy[2]

Credits

1 Mark Pepper   3 Peter Bentley
2 Barry Pickthall   4 Cedric Robertson

All other photographs were taken by the author

CHARTS

The Global Challenge 20–21

Southampton to Cape Horn 40

Approaching the Horn 72

Cape Horn to Hobart 76

Passing South Island, New Zealand 106

Hobart to the Cape of Good Hope 116

Cape of Good Hope to Southampton 148

Charts devised by Captain Spencer Drummond
with route plotting supplied by BT
and drawn by ML Design

Forepeak
(*Stowage for sails in
regular use*)   Sail Hatch   Toilet/Shower   Vang Strut

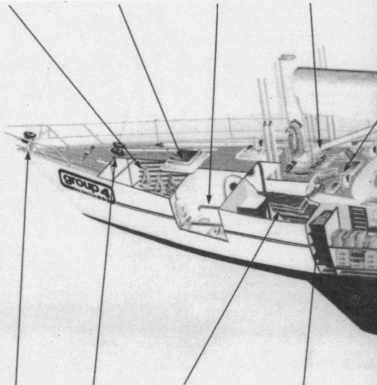

Furling   Furling   Double Cabins   Storage
Headsail   Staysail   (*Filled with spare sails   Rack
                                and equipment*)

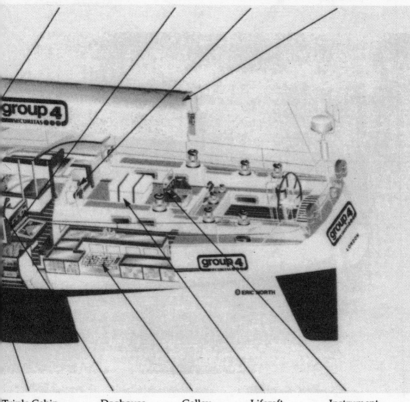

Mast Deckplate
With   3 mainsail reefing pennants
and outhaul
8 halyards   Navigation   Fully Battened
Cunningham control   Station   Mainsail with
mechanical vang control   Main Hatch   Lazy jacks

Triple Cabin   Doghouse   Galley   Liferaft   Instrument
(Bunks used for   Berth   Stowage   Displays
storage)

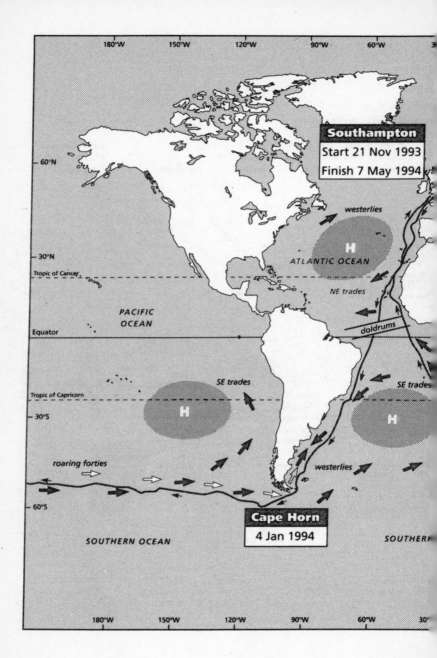

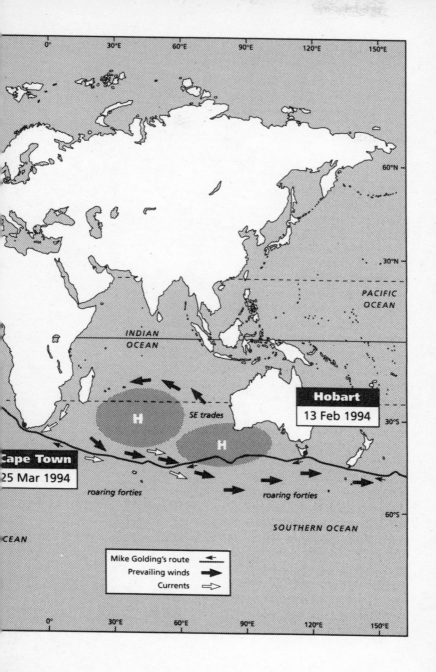

Hobart
13 Feb 1994

Cape Town
25 Mar 1994

INDIAN
OCEAN

PACIFIC
OCEAN

SE trades

roaring forties   roaring forties

SOUTHERN OCEAN

CEAN

Mike Golding's route
Prevailing winds
Currents

INTRODUCTION

by Jørgen Philip-Sørensen
Chairman and Chief Executive,
Group 4 Securitas (International)

WHEN Chay Blyth completed his incredible feat of sailing single-handed, non-stop around the world from east-to-west (the difficult way!) in 1971 he became a national hero. He was the first person ever to complete the so-called 'impossible voyage' which ensured that his name would be added to the list of the world's other great solo sailors, such as Sir Francis Chichester and Sir Alec Rose.

The achievement of each enthralled us, but it is Chay Blyth's which I remember most vividly, perhaps because – with his usual talent for being in the right place at the right time – Chay's return coincided with Cowes Week and so he was greeted by various members of the Royal Family and the prime minister of the day, Ted Heath, all of whom were keen sailors. It was a triumphant homecoming, shared with millions through live television coverage.

Whereas Chichester and Rose had both broken their journeys at the halfway stage, in Australia, Chay made his voyage without stopping, despite the fact that he was sailing against the prevailing winds and currents.

Chay has remained one of my heroes ever since and I was particularly delighted to be able to start working with him early in the 1990s in realising his ambition to stage a race of identical, all-steel yachts crewed by amateurs. The idea immediately appealed to me and it came at a time when my company was looking for a marketing strategy to emphasise its international growth. Sponsorship of a yacht in the race was perfect for the promotion we had in mind and it also had the advantage of being an exciting adventure in which Group 4, as a company, could participate.

I had decided, at an early stage, that I would like four of our employees to join the other twelve volunteers on the yacht – one on each leg – and this created a keen interest in the adventure among the 40,000 people who work for us around the world. My desire to involve the whole Group 4 'family' also resulted in what must have been one of the strangest yacht-naming ceremonies of all time. While other sponsors named their yachts on the water, *Group 4* was taken inland, to the centre of England, to our Broadway, Worcester, offices overlooking the Vale of Evesham and named, by my grand-daughter, Ingrid, at a height of 750 feet above sea level.

As a sponsor there were many ways in which we could take advantage of our participation in the British Steel Challenge Race, as the yacht sailed first from Southampton to Rio de Janeiro, then on to Hobart, Tasmania, followed by Cape Town, South Africa, before returning home. Our businesses in South America and Australasia made the stopovers in those ports even more enjoyable for the crew and their supporters.

But there were a number of elements over which we had no control: notably the choice of skipper and crew. It was, therefore, our great good fortune that fireman Mike Golding was assigned by Chay to skipper *Group 4*. And the rest of the crew proved to be equally excellent ambassadors of Group 4 as they sailed the world. I am proud to say that they also became my friends and their return was a very emotional experience for me and my colleagues.

The other elements beyond our control, of course, were the incredible seas and appalling weather which the yacht encountered at various stages in her voyage. All we could do, as we followed her progress on the positional maps sent back by satellite and received telexes telling us how they were coping, was to send words of encouragement and hope for their safe and speedy return.

What Mike Golding demonstrated on that voyage was his superb leadership qualities – something he had little opportunity to do in the single-handed and short-handed sailing events in which he had previously competed. Despite a major setback soon after setting out from Rio de Janeiro, which put *Group 4* out of the race for forty-eight hours as the other yachts sailed on, Mike and his crew succeeded not only in winning two of the four legs of the race (which no other boat achieved) but also in coming in second, just seventy minutes behind the overall winner.

Our involvement in the race led me to make two important decisions. The first was to buy the yacht from Chay Blyth's Challenge Business because, having been so involved with her from before she even went into the water, I could not bear to think of her carrying anyone else's name. Part of the agreement was that she will sail in the next round-the-world race which Chay is organising for 1996.

I also asked Mike Golding to join our organisation and run a new company I had formed, Group 4 PromOcean, involving outward-bound-style management training centred on the yacht. Mike's leadership qualities made him the ideal candidate for the job and I was delighted when he accepted.

But I confess the next twist in the story took me totally by surprise. Mike Golding came to see me one day and cautiously but confidently outlined a bold plan. He wanted to try to beat Chay Blyth's record which had stood far longer than anyone had expected. Would I agree to let him alter the 67-foot, all-steel boat, making her suitable for single-handed sailing, and take her around the world again?

It is a measure of my confidence in Mike and *Group 4* that I gave him the go ahead in a matter of days, after consultations with my directors and the man who would lose his record if Mike succeeded in his attempt – Chay Blyth. They all thought it a splendid idea.

As a result, we decided to establish the Group 4 Global Challenge Award to be presented to whoever holds the fastest solo record for sailing non-stop the 'wrong' way around the world. Naturally, we hoped that our own man would be the first to receive it but we also knew that it was going to be far from easy. The fact that the record had stood for nearly a quarter of a century, despite a number of attempts, confirmed that.

The rest, as they say, is history . . . which Mike Golding has rewritten so brilliantly with his epic voyage.

JPS
Broadway, July 1994

1

A Hidden Agenda

Group 4 fell off steep waves with sickening frequency, the shock reverberating through the steel hull and into the very souls of all fourteen crew members. At a quarter to midnight I climbed into a damp sleeping bag, exhausted from several hours on deck in freezing conditions. We were four days out on leg two of the British Steel Challenge Race and at last our crew seemed to be getting it together. When I had come below, *Nuclear Electric*, the leading yacht, was just visible off the port quarter. Sleet and rain, driven by 30 knots of wind, made looking for her sting the eyes, the water pummelled exposed skin. The on watch now had their work cut out trying to pass her whilst smashing to windward in the short freezing seas that thundered up from the south. The off watch lay in their bunks, trying to get circulation back into hands and feet before the next call on deck.

Moments later a loud crack had me and those around me leaping for our foul-weather clothing, a deafening flapping sound signalled a major problem. I rushed on deck as quickly as possible, shouting for the boat to be brought off the wind. When I looked up the mast it was clear something was badly wrong. Through the blackness in the wavering light of a torch, the top of the spar lurched around unsupported. Only by coming off the wind was the top section saved from complete failure. Waves broke clear over the bows as four of us worked our way forward into the glow of the deck lights. Spray and spume flew horizontally across the lit deck area as we struggled to find exactly what had failed.

Unbelievably, the 14 mm forestay bottlescrew had snapped clean across the threaded portion. The yankee headsail had been torn in two right through the heavily reinforced tack and clew and the broken stay was snaking through the air, driven by the uncontrolled power of 1000 square feet of sail. If it so much as touched anyone they would at best be seriously hurt, at worst knocked clean over the side or decapitated. In minutes the whole crew was on deck and struggling to bring the sail down, attaching spinnaker halyards to the stem fitting to support the masthead. Very little had been said, the incident demonstrated teamwork at its best.

We could only watch as the lights of the other yachts passed us one by one. With the situation back under control, it began to sink in that this one incident could put us out of the running for the rest of the race. The questioning faces of the crew said it all. As far as the race was concerned, surely we could not recover from this? Prior to my selection as the skipper of *Group 4* for the British Steel Challenge Race, my experience had been predominantly either single- or short-handed sailing. As I struggled and sweated with the others to get the destroyed sail below deck I couldn't have foreseen that just one year later, almost to the day, I would set out to sail *Group 4* alone around the world.

Five months later on 23rd May the crew had turned disaster into victory. *Group 4* sailed triumphantly up the Solent towards the finish. Despite having had a second forestay failure less than 3,000 miles after the first, they had shown true grit, driving on through the Southern Ocean to arrive fifth in Hobart. They then went on to win outright the two following legs to Cape Town and now back into the Solent. If *Nuclear Electric*, who as we approached the line were still battling against strong currents in light airs off St Albans Head, took over seven hours more than us to finish, we would receive the British Steel Challenge Trophy. However, they crossed the line after six hours in a brilliant display of sailing in difficult conditions. The crew of *Group 4* were not to be phased. Coming from behind, they had missed out on an overall win by just seventy minutes. We celebrated our successes rather than ponder on our failures.

Over the next few days one by one all the Challenge yachts arrived back in Southampton. The crews had completed the adventure of a lifetime and now began to disperse back to normal life. For some it would prove more difficult than others. Racing around the world is an unsettling affair at the best of times. Those who had given up a great deal – jobs, houses and relationships – to take part in the race were to find it difficult to pick up the pieces. I was more lucky. I had been granted a leave of absence from my job as a Watch Commander with Royal Berkshire Fire and Rescue Service to compete in the Challenge Race.

The Chairman of Group 4, Jørgen Philip-Sørensen, was much more than the boat's backer. He had become personally involved with the trials and tribulations of the crew. Despite his impressive work schedule, he was present to welcome us with his support and encouragement into each port of call, his enthusiasm for the event and his crew seemed limitless. Philip is a unique entrepreneur. A Swede, born in Denmark, at one point he was selling security during the day and standing as a guard during the night. Now Group 4 is one of the largest security organisations in the world, employing 40,000 people in thirty countries. At fifty-five Philip retains full private control of Group 4, he loves to know what is going on in every area and his involvement with the Challenge Race was little different.

A few days after the finish he approached me with some surprising news. Group 4 had bought the yacht from the Challenge Business and planned to set up a company to run personal development and team skills courses. He outlined his plans and went on to offer me a position as general manager responsible for developing the new activities and administering the yacht. It was a fascinating new opportunity, a complete change of direction with a company I had grown to respect for their professionalism in all things. I accepted immediately.

Michael O'Regan (universally known as Sumo) and Martin Hall, two of the Challenge crew members, joined me in the new company – Group 4 PromOcean. Within two weeks of our return we were all heavily engaged in our new activities. Over the next few months the boat toured Sweden, Holland and Belgium on a series of events. We were still planning the new training courses and our activities were primarily post-race PR events. The Challenge Race had created enormous interest in the crews and the yachts. Martin, Sumo and I often delivered the boat to each venue. Following a particularly hospitable hospitality session with

Group 4 Belgium, the crew felt exhausted on the sail from Antwerp back to Solent for Cowes Week. I however felt okay and overnight I sailed the boat alone. It was easy sailing and not very testing, but by morning I had begun to evolve the idea of taking *Group 4* westabout around the world, non-stop and alone.

In late September I was due to attend a meeting at Group 4's HQ at Broadway. Several of the key people within the company wanted to hear more about the development plans for PromOcean. I had produced an agenda to guide us through the various parts of the meeting – Chay had once told the skippers, 'He who controls the agenda controls the meeting.' Before this meeting I had the agenda copied for all the people due to attend. The last item on the list was 'The Group 4 Global Challenge: an attempt on the solo westabout circumnavigation record.' Another gem that Chay impressed on the skippers was to 'always have a hidden agenda'. My courage wavered at the last moment and I whited my last item out, recopying the agenda and moving the Global Challenge into my hidden agenda. I wanted to gauge reactions before suggesting such a radical idea.

Nearing the end of the meeting we had arrived at an impasse. Concepts for the training courses were coming together well, but the winter months ahead were not a good time to be starting the training activities we were planning. We also wanted to research the course content more thoroughly, so it seemed we would not realistically be ready to operate as a training company until the spring of 1994. As a result there was going to be a slack period over the winter months – a perfect opportunity to introduce the idea of Global Challenge had developed. Coffee arrived and several people left the room. Two with whom I had worked closely on the Challenge Race, Loek Malemberg and Charles Rice, remained. In a casual way I broached the idea of setting out to beat Chay's record, almost joking but watching the faces closely for their reactions. Looks of surprise and amusement changed rapidly to those of interest and searching questions arrived thick and fast. I outlined a rough plan of what would be needed to convert the yacht to one capable of being sailed solo, together with a proposed date for a start from the Solent. Their response encouraged me to put more detailed plans together and approach Philip Sørensen for the ultimate sanction.

Philip's reaction was remarkably controlled. He couldn't believe that I really wanted to do something so extreme but from his response I suspected that he had half-expected to hear me suggest something like this. As we talked, I could not prevent myself becoming over-enthusiastic. I had not raised my hopes until now, but Philip's reaction was so immediately positive that it was a job for me to quell a growing excitement. It was going to be a tough decision for him to make. Group 4 is a very high-profile company, operating in many sensitive areas. The thrust of their business is about safety and security. For them to support a venture which would be perceived by some as unnecessarily dangerous held considerable corporate risks. As Chief Executive of a private company Philip could only make this decision alone.

Two days later we spoke again. 'Are really sure that this is what you want to do?' he asked. I explained that I really did want to go out and give it my best shot because I was sure I could do it. But if anything went seriously wrong, or I felt I was in over my head, I promised I would stop. I was not going sailing to die, only to do the best I could at establishing a new record. He seemed more satisfied by this and was soon giving his unreserved support for the venture.

When I telephoned Chay Blyth in September with the news that I planned to have a crack at his record, it was hard to gauge what his reaction might be. As the figurehead and organiser of the British Steel Challenge Race Chay had been responsible for the construction of the boat I was to use in the attempt, as well as for introducing me to Group 4. Unknowingly, he had placed at my disposal everything that would be needed in an attempt to better his time and establish a new westabout record.

Chay is seldom phased and perhaps, predictably, his immediate reaction was typically unpredictable. 'Great, I love it!' he said. 'The best projects always start this way. I'm off down the pub, call you in an hour to discuss it.' I was dumbfounded at how quickly the call was over, but at least he seemed positive. Sure enough, he called back an hour later, having obviously made some notes for my benefit. He was enthusiastic and behind the project and offered the full support of the Challenge Race support team.

So the count down had started. There were just six weeks to modify, prepare, victual and test *Group 4* for what I estimated to be voyage of around 180 days. 'If this whole thing is possible,' I said, 'it's possible to prepare for it in six weeks.' I hoped I was right! Group 4 commissioned a new perpetual trophy for the record. The Group 4 Global Challenge Trophy was to be kept a closely guarded secret until just ten days before the start. This would forestall any others from setting out on the same record before us and it would provide a better impact to release all the details in a controlled way and with the yacht prepared and modified for the purpose.

The 21st November was the date that I had planned to leave. It is important to pick the right time of year in order to arrive in the Southern Ocean in the southern summer. Too early or too late would reduce the chances of success and make any attempt far more dangerous. Estimating how long it would take to reach various points along the course was made simpler by the experience of the previous year's race and, although I was leaving later than the Challenge Race had, I reckoned that sailing alone would reduce my speed by around ten per cent. Based on this, and subtracting the stopover periods, I should arrive at the Cape of Good Hope at around the same time of year as the Challenge boats had, late March – assuming of course all went as planned.

Group 4 was designed by David Thomas as one of the ten 67-foot British Steel Challenge yachts. With a mild steel hull and a stainless steel deck, she is rigged as a Bermudan cutter with as much as 4700 square feet of downwind sail area. The boats were designed to be handled by a crew of fourteen and were never intended to be sailed short-handed, never mind single-handed. In assessing what modifications would be needed to make the boat manageable alone, we needed to bear in mind simplicity and the need to return the yacht to its full one-design specification when the attempt was over. I ruled out major changes which sprang to mind. They would take too long, cost too much and, because any modification would be untested offshore, would present too great a risk of failure on what was otherwise a proven design.

These limitations actually made the modification process very simple. I chose to concentrate modifications in three main areas – rethinking the sail-handling, adding an autopilot system and improving the efficiency of the power generation system. Together with

Andrew Roberts, the Project Manager for the Challenge Business, we began discussions with the companies who would supply and fit new equipment. We naturally gravitated towards those with proven track records who had been involved with supplying the Challenge Race, as they would understand what the equipment needed to be capable of putting up with – sailing westabout puts enormous strain on gear which would otherwise last a yacht's lifetime.

Seemingly endless lists of things to do started to build up. I slept with a note pad by my bed. We divided the six weeks into three two-week periods for researching new equipment and regular refit work, fitting new equipment and sailing trials, and the Global Challenge Trophy announcement. It was a simple plan, but no matter how much preparation time is allocated, the final weeks of preparation inevitably become a frantic scrabble.

Group 4 was lifted out of the water and her mast removed at Shamrock Quay, Southampton. Since returning from the race four months before, the boat had had no more than a cursory looking over. To sail around again, without stops or assistance, everything would need to be even more reliable than during the Challenge. In that race three ports of call gave opportunities for repair and revictualling. From the moment I left the Solent I would need to have either total reliability or the ability to fix any serious problem myself. To stop or take outside aid, in whatever form, would invalidate the record attempt. The rules governing round-the-world records are laid down by the WSSRC, the World Speed Sailing Record Council, who also provide observers to time yachts in and out and monitor any attempts. Their rules state:

Single-handed means there is only one person on board. If a single-handed skipper accepts any form of outside assistance then the voyage is no longer considered single-handed. Every single-handed record attempt is assumed to be without assistance.

Without assistance means that a vessel may not receive any kind of outside assistance whatever, nor take on board any supplies, materials or equipment during a record attempt. A crew might decide to anchor or even to beach their craft for repairs but, if so, they must do so entirely without help. It is permitted to drop items such as film or tape for recovery but nothing is to be taken on board. In the event of fouling another craft or obstruction, eg an oil rig, it is permitted for the crew of the other craft or structure to assist the vessel in getting clear. Outside weather information is permitted.

To circumnavigate a vessel must start and finish from the same point, it must cross all meridians of longitude and the equator, it may cut some meridians more than once but not all of them (eg two laps of Antarctica is not allowed). The straight line track of the vessel must be at least 21,600 miles in length (in the case of a westabout circumnavigation it is likely that a vessel will clock of nearer 30,000 miles).

By the start of the second week *Group 4* was in pieces and Sumo, Martin and Andrew Roberts did their best to keep me away from the yacht. The support crew often worked from the early hours until late into the night, trying to meet near impossible deadlines and I knew how fortunate I was to have such committed people doing the work. I was allowed to show my face in the evening to go through any problems that had come up during the day. As time went on I became increasingly nervous that we were trying to do too much, that the boat had been stripped down too far. We carried out non-destructive testing on all of the rigging bottlescrews and fittings and this had meant spreading the work between several workshops all along the south coast.

Deadlines were constantly foiled by the unexpected. The day before the boat was due to be re-launched four of us struggled to remove the prop. shaft to replace the deep-sea seal. We got the shaft to a point of no return but nothing we did would shift the coupling on the inboard end. Eventually, a local engineering shop was called in to remove the fitting. Hydraulic jacks from all around the yard, steadily increasing in size, were brought to bear on it. Each time, just as it seemed it was about to break free, the rams would fail, pouring gallons of hydraulic oil round the engine room. By late afternoon we had broken every hydraulic jack available in Southampton. Huge oxy-acetylene gear was heaved up on deck and down below the fitting was heated until cherry red. Still it seemed stuck in place. We had begun to plan to cut it free and replace the whole shaft by the time it finally gave way to some brutal hammering, levering and jacking. Shortly after midnight we had it all reassembled ready for an early morning launch.

I had finally settled on one company to supply the entire autopilot system. Autohelm had supplied the existing instrument system and I had used their pilots successfully before. They were the obvious choice and their product support team, led by Steve Moore, was second to none. This was one of the few companies who knew what the boat was about to do as they had been closely involved with the previous year's race. Work began to fit the system, with engineers and electricians climbing over each other in a bid to get their work completed on schedule. All the wiring runs were labelled and a master diagram was produced; if anything went wrong I would need to be able to find where wires went to and from.

Peter Vroon of Hoods Sailmaker was very enthusiastic from the outset. Hoods had built the sails for the Challenge Race and now went about the process of converting the sail plan to one capable of being handled alone. The new sail plan included a fully battened mainsail with a Frederiksen external track and ball-bearing cars which were fitted into the existing luff groove in the mast (without needing to drill any holes). The new headsails were designed to be used on their own roller furling gear. The yankee was just slightly bigger than the existing No 1 yankee, closer in area to the genoa but more adaptable, with the ability to part furl the sail. For very light airs I had a lightweight multi-purpose genoa (MPG), stored on its own flexible furling system, which could be coiled down below ready for use. Many of the original sails were converted for use with the new system and were carried as spares. Three spinnakers – a light, asymmetric and a new short luffed heavyweight – were fitted into spinnaker socks. The result was not only capable of being handled by one man, but it was also a more powerful arrangement.

The main engine was the only way of charging the batteries during the Challenge Race. Two 110 amp MOD, standard 24 volt alternators, as well as a watermaker pump, were driven off a Ford Mermaid 135 hp engine. This had proved very reliable but the fuel consumption was far too high for a non-stop voyage around the world, especially with the additional load of the autopilot motor. We settled on supplementing the existing set up with a small but sophisticated diesel generator which was fitted into the foulies locker. This would need running for up to eight hours a day but the fuel consumption was still scarcely a quarter of that of the main engine. I hoped that this would offer virtually unlimited power supplies, as well as providing a 110 volt DC supply to run a power drill and power the camera lighting.

For communications we chose to stick with the existing single sideband radio (SSB) and the Mascot standard 'C' telex equipment. Telexes could be sent to and from the boat via the Inmarsat satellite. This equipment was interfaced with one of the GPS (Global Positioning System) units to provide position fixes to Global Challenge Control which was to be based at Group 4's permanently manned Broadway headquarters. BT developed a program which would enable the day to day tracking of the yacht to be displayed on a suitably equipped computer screen, together with comparative data and tracks from past events. Both Chay's and my track, for example, could be displayed together.

I approached two of *Group 4*'s former crew members, Don Deakin and David Cowan, in the hope they would help me compile a food and consumable supplies list. In the event they unselfishly took on the huge job of listing, buying and arranging a storage system for all the victuals. I had made the decision to avoid freeze-dried food in favour of the type of long-life food one finds in the supermarkets. If I was to spend so long at sea the comfort factor would be very important and these dishes were easily cooked and generally very high quality. Don and I sat down one morning for a mammoth tasting session. In the event I was pushed for time and many of the choices were made on the basis of the packaging picture, something I would live to regret.

The departure date approached like a train. The lists of things to do remained as long as ever but by now the items were becoming less essential. The regular support crew swelled with more ex-crew members from the Challenge Race and slowly but surely the jobs lists shrank. On the day of the press launch, just ten days before I was due to start, one of the most frequently asked questions was: had I tried to sail the boat alone? In the interests of appearing better prepared than we actually were, I replied, with my fingers crossed, that I had and the trials had gone well. In one way I was telling the truth, for there was not a day in the past six weeks when I had not in my mind been practising every manoeuvre with every sail, in every situation. The sober truth was that the boat had not even been out sailing since the refit, never mind solo.

When we finally did get out, a full support crew was on board, hiding below when photos were taken, but on deck whenever any serious manoeuvring took place in the confines of the Solent. I tacked the boat alone twice during that day, with everyone watching me struggle and sweat to winch in the huge yankee headsail. I put on a brave face and hoped the audience felt more confident of the success of the project than I did at that moment.

Finally departure day arrived.

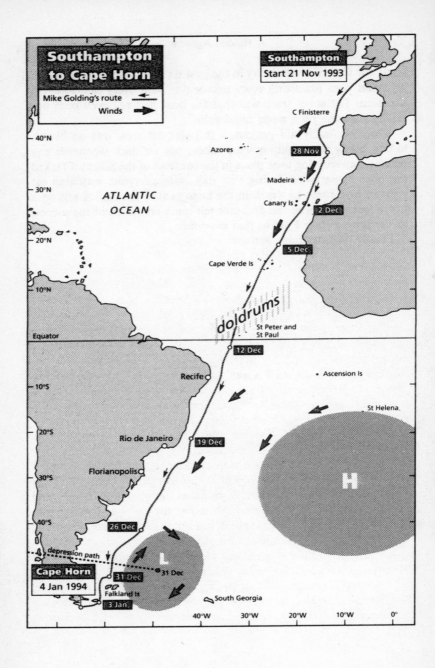

Southampton to Cape Horn

Mike Golding's route ·······►
Winds ➡

Southampton
Start 21 Nov 1993

40°N
C Finisterre
28 Nov
Azores
Madeira
30°N
ATLANTIC OCEAN
Canary Is
2 Dec
20°N
5 Dec
Cape Verde Is
10°N
doldrums
St Peter and St Paul
Equator
12 Dec
Ascension Is
10°S
Recife
St Helena
20°S
Rio de Janeiro
19 Dec
Florianopolis
30°S
H
26 Dec
40°S
depression path
L
31 Dec
Cape Horn
4 Jan 1994
31 Dec
Falkland Is
3 Jan
South Georgia
40°W   30°W   20°W   10°W   0°

2

One Day at a Time
(Day 1 – Day 17)

Departure day was full of strange feelings. I woke early, having slept well, dressed, joked with my girlfriend Ceri about just popping out for a sail, and headed for Ocean Village Marina and my home for six months, *Group 4*. When I arrived Charles Rice had the few hours that remained before the start all programmed and in a dreamlike state I fielded repeated questions about how I felt, uncertain of the truth of my answers.

In reality I felt very little. I was nervous of the start but also looking forward to getting on with the job. Only then would I begin to know if what I had been claiming I could do for the past six weeks was really possible. In many respects the people who had gathered to see me off were probably thinking further ahead than I was. Already I was operating in a one day at a time mode.

The gods smiled on *Group 4*, and a gentle easterly breeze allowed a trouble-free sail out of the Solent. I thought about flying the huge 3780-square foot promotional spinnaker to give my friends and supporters a bit of a show to remember me by. But caution prevailed. I was very aware that I had still not actually hoisted the thing alone before. For that matter I'd not sailed *Group 4* solo yet. So the risk of a highly public foul up was too high. The objective was to get clear safely and that needed all my concentration.

As *Group 4* and the fleet of support boats made their way out of the Solent I needed to gybe several times, at one point narrowly avoiding a collision with the main support boat whose skipper, possibly distracted by the noise from 250 supporters, seemed unaware of my need to work the fickle winds. Above all the background din I could distinctly recognise some of Chay's sharper tones making it clear who he felt should be keeping clear of whom.

Clear of the Needles, the fleet of supporters drew close one by one and, after cheers and waves, each boat turned and headed back towards Southampton. Eventually *Group 4* and I were alone together and, as night drew in, the first glimmering understanding of the full magnitude of the challenge that lay ahead made itself felt as I put the first of thousands of reefs into the mainsail and *Group 4*, with the bit between her teeth, kicked spray over the foredeck. It had been a fantastic day, with friends travelling from all over the country to see me off. It was enough to make me wonder why in hell I wanted to undertake six months of solitude. The truth is I was not seeking solitude, only the record.

That night was spent busily dodging shipping in the English Channel as I made my way to the first corner at Ushant. Worried about the prospect of a collision, I stayed awake all night and the following day. The busy shipping lanes of the Channel were one of the more trying parts of the whole passage. At the same time I couldn't help but feel a sense of anticlimax. The frantic preparations and huge workloads of the previous six weeks were over. It scarcely seemed possible that we had turned the yacht around in such a short time. Everyone had worked flat out and, although I was fairly confident that nothing had been forgotten, I watched the unproven new equipment hawkishly. The multitude of things that had been of concern during the weeks of preparation were now reduced to the relatively simple concerns of the wind, the sea and the yacht.

By the morning of the 22nd November, on a crisp blue skied winter's day, the weather was settled enough for me to try the spinnaker. The task of hauling and winching the sail, in its sock (which weighs more than a small motor bike), up the eighty-five-foot mast had me gasping for air. The pole could only be lifted one end at a time and needed to be winched into position.

Very slowly and double-checking everything I got it up and was rewarded by it opening with a satisfying crack as it filled and *Group 4* surged forward towards Biscay and warmer climes. Pete Goss, the

Challenge training skipper, was trying to rendezvous with me as I left the Channel, but with a freshening breeze and *Group 4* sailing at hull speed under spinnaker, it was going to be impossible for the training yacht to catch me. This was the beginning, no more waving goodbyes. It was time to get cracking.

There was only one niggle to spoil this up, up and away mood. During the day the autopilot kicked off twice. We had not had time to test the system fully before departure. Perhaps an Atlantic crossing would have been the only way to do that. I was convinced it was a simple wiring fault, but I was unable to find anything obvious. I had specified the Autohelm/Raytheon autopilot system because I felt it was the best for the job, but this early glitch was worrying. When the system was being fitted I had had long sessions with Autohelm's Steve Moore. We both knew how crucial its reliability would be to my success but, equally, we both knew that the voyage I was undertaking was going to test any autopilot system way beyond the regular call of duty. I persuaded Steve this was not the opportunity for them to test new equipment and made sure Autohelm fitted hydraulic ram units of proven design. They also set up a mirror pilot system in their factory on which they could monitor any problems that might occur along the way. This was later to prove a godsend. Because the autopilot problem was only occurring every twelve hours or so, I tried to trace it by disconnecting the various control heads one by one in order to isolate the faulty component – it was to take several weeks and hundreds of variations before I found the cause. Who needs executive toys to help pass the time at sea?

In the evening, when the wind began to freshen and veer, I took the spinnaker down and unfurled the headsail, and as the wind continued to increase I began a long night's work changing down through the various sail plans, which was my first chance to try all the new equipment under load. At 0200 on the 23rd, I went below, having furled the headsail completely and put the second reef in the mainsail. The wind was up to 30 knots and *Group 4* was crashing to windward in freezing conditions, snow sprinkling the decks, while below I stripped out of sweat-soaked clothing. Reefing was proving to be hard work.

Suddenly, the frightening sound of water surging through the bilges had me hurriedly lifting all the access hatches along the main companionway. The bilges were full and getting fuller. In the red glow of the emergency night lights I inspected all the obvious places for water to enter the boat, by way of the variety of fittings which pass through the hull, but this did not reveal anything. By now I needed to pump the forward section manually. When I had got the water down to a reasonable level, I began a second systematic check of the seacocks. Water was still pouring in from somewhere.

There are fifteen designed holes in *Group 4*'s hull, each with a shut-off valve, which allow water in and waste/exhaust out of the yacht. I checked them all, not an easy task as many are difficult to access, especially at night bashing to windward with half the fittings beneath the slowly rising water. Still no leaks were visible! Next I checked all the joints and connecting pipes, of which there are hundreds. After a worrying period of pumping and searching I eventually found the source. A half-inch tank breather pipe had fallen off, allowing sea water to enter under pressure. After shutting it down, I again pumped the bilges and collapsed exhausted but highly relieved in the navigation station. Minutes later the wind rose further to 40 knots and I was again on deck, fighting and sweating to put the deep reef in the mainsail.

Three days out and finally things began to settle down. I was able to sleep in short spells as the shipping traffic eased and *Group 4* headed west through Biscay. A full comprehension of what Global Challenge was going to mean began to dawn on me – with only six weeks to prepare there had been little time for real mental preparation. I still felt happy enough, so long as I didn't think of the whole six months ahead of me – just one day at a time.

Gradually, I was getting opportunities to test and practise with the new sails, furling systems and autopilot. For light airs beating and reaching I had a new lightweight genoa (MPG) and on day 4 I tested this for the first time. Keeping a thirty-eight ton (laden) Challenge yacht moving in light conditions had always proved difficult, but the MPG certainly made a difference. With a cloth weight of 2.2 ounces the sail would fill and set in the lightest of winds. The MPG was stored on a wire furling gear and could be hoisted on a halyard and unfurled and furled with great ease. This sail helped the yacht through periods of light weather and improved performance overall.

On the weekend of the 27th and 28th I had the yacht bashing to windward in a gale, which was good experience for the Southern Ocean. During this period my main problem was managing to get enough sleep. I knew I had to establish some kind of regular system. But I probably slept for about four hours in the twenty-four for many days and the amount of shipping around didn't help. I was becoming increasingly tired.

The new design of the furling headsail needed different treatment to the original Challenge Race arrangement. The problem was that when the yankee was part furled the sail area was set too high, giving the sail a fuller, more powerful shape. This meant that in winds of over 24 knots *Group 4* would lie over on her side and slam badly. The only way to reduce this unproductive slamming was to wind the whole sail away and use just the staysail and a double reefed mainsail. Initially, I felt guilty that I was not trying hard enough when this slower rig was set, but there were no other options and I would pray for a change in strength when the wind was between 24 and 28 knots. Eventually, these constantly changing winds and periods of slow weather gave way to the north-east trade winds and I was soon surfing down steep seas in 35–40 knots of wind – boat speed 11 knots – with a poled out yankee, one reef in the mainsail and in control . . . just!

The weather quickly became warmer. Grey skies were replaced by beautiful blue horizons with long fluffy lines of cumulus, following the steady progress of the trades. Then, crisis – during a gybe the yankee became wrapped so tightly around the forestay in a devious double/triple twist that it defied any sensible attempt to unwind it. It would not come down or furl and to cure the problem meant my first scary trip up the forestay on my self-ascending kit (a four-to-one block and tackle). After five hours working in darkness and still ploughing towards the Canaries at over 7 knots under a full moon, with the yacht a mass of tangled rope and cloth, I physically pulled the sail round and round the stay until it was clear.

As I had anticipated from the Challenge Race, downwind sailing was going to be the Achilles heel of sailing solo with *Group 4*. But regardless of the difficulties, day to day progress was good and solid in the trade winds. I had by now experienced virtually all manner of conditions and had every variety of sail plan working at one time or other. The 24-knot limit for carrying headsails seemed the only poor plan and was to prove more frustrating in the Southern Ocean where the wind strength was often in this range.

Adrian Donovan, the skipper of *Heath Insured* during the British Steel Challenge, was in the Canaries sailing the yacht *Craftman's Art*, bound for the Caribbean. As I closed with the islands, we communicated regularly by Inmarsat and in the first of several coincidences he became involved with the rendezvous carrying out the film crew and picking up the film and video footage from my first few weeks.

At dawn on 2nd December, twelve days out, the mountainous shapes of Gran Canaria appeared ahead. Tenerife was just visible in the sea-level morning haze. Steep blue seas gave me some exciting surfing as I searched with binoculars for *Craftman's Art* and the camera crew. It was wonderful to see friendly and familiar faces. Although I had only been at sea for two weeks, I was really still coming to terms with being alone on *Group 4*. I still woke occasionally expecting to find the familiar faces of my Challenge crew busy working the boat.

We chatted on the radio as *Craftman's Art* circled *Group 4* filming and photographing the yacht forging south against the steep backdrop of the west coast of the island. After taking my first film canister back to shore, the film crew returned for further filming and photography in a light aircraft. By the time they arrived I was totally worn out and frustrated after trying to set a spinnaker, only to find a series of wind shifts caused by the turbulence in the lee of the island had forced me to gybe the boat several times – each manoeuvre involving twenty hard, hot and sweaty minutes of work. Eventually I gave up the effort and resorted back to the normal fore and aft sails. Even thirty miles away the wind in the lee of the island was still gusty and all over the place.

My track was now further east than I would have liked. The constantly shifting winds to leeward of the Canaries kept me very busy gybing back and forth and trying to stay on the favoured gybe. Ahead of me the Cape Verdes lay directly in my path and, despite my best efforts to push west, the weather was now forcing me towards a track which passed between the islands.

Once the wind settled back into the steady trade winds, I took the opportunity to give the sails a good inspection. After a couple of weeks' use the sails had settled down and showed some early signs of chafe in leech lines, in particular the leather-clad leech line pocket on the yankee. I took all the sails down and inspected them, repairing various small problems, rectifying the causes and replacing the leech line in the mainsail. With the doldrums ahead now I tried to plan the quickest route through them. I aimed to cross at around 32° West, both the statistically thinnest point and, according to the data from weatherfaxes, the best chance of a smooth passage through the infamous band of light winds and squalls.

By now I had established a regular pattern to my days. I had been writing up my diary daily and sending short reports back to Group 4 on the Inmarsat system. I decided that it made sense to write my diary straight on to the Inmarsat and send it as a more informative daily report. I liked doing it this way as I could type it into the machine and hit the send button, committing my thoughts and feelings in a way that I could not edit and rewrite. I hoped that in doing it this way Group 4 and all the people following my progress would get a better insight into the ups and downs of solo sailing. I had been so busy learning the practical things about sailing such a big yacht alone I had had little time for introspection. In general I liked it that way – you can think too much in my situation. Later, once the practical problems of running the boat became more routine, I tried to convert this single-mindedness into boat speed and already I felt really bad and hurt if I knew I had missed any opportunities to make extra progress. Later this feeling was to become a real driving force, as well as the source of many frustrations.

On 5th December my first daily report was sent:

The last 48 hrs have been wonderful trade wind sailing weather, steadily NE winds are pushing *Group 4* straight down the line towards Cape Horn. The rendezvous at the Canaries has pinned my course too far to the east and I am now trying to push west to cross the equator at 32° West. Cape Verde Islands are right on my course line. To avoid them I am pinching even further west every time the wind veers and allows me.

Last night the wind was up to 25–30 knots for a few hours, beyond the limit I had set for flying the spinnaker whilst solo. *Group 4*'s spinnaker can only be flown from the masthead – making it a huge sail for one man to get up and, more importantly, down. But, I could not resist sailing the boat on the short surfing waves for several hours until the wind eased back at 0400 this morning. The autopilot copes well, even in surfing conditions, providing it's calibrated for the conditions and the sails are well trimmed to reduce the load on the steering. To achieve this I will normally steer the yacht for a period, to check the balance, after every sail change or re-trimming. The wind built up again this morning and I re-trimmed the spinnaker. Making the shape flatter to depower the sail, I grabbed the helm and pressed standby on the starboard pilot – to take control. The pilot stopped, as it should, but the wheel was still locked – the hydraulic bypass valve had stuck.

Group 4 broached wildly, pinning the yacht down on her starboard side with the boom well in the water and the spinnaker doing its level best to break the pole. This was visibly bending under the shock loads of the spinnaker collapsing and refilling with loud crashes. I went below and switched to the port pilot, and grabbed some tools. The port pilot ram did not have the power to push against the jammed starboard unit, so I re-engaged the starboard pilot and reset the course.

Group 4 lifted her boom clear of the water and bolted off downwind at 11 knots. After twenty minutes I had the starboard pilot working again, having opened the relief valve with the aid of a judicious clout from one of my favourite tools, a big club hammer. I've left the ram disconnected and will seek advice from Autohelm before I attempt a repair.

Ironically, this first report encapsulated many of the problems that were to plague me in the months ahead. There would be the frustration when I felt I should be sailing on a different track or in any way at less than her optimum speed; there was the trouble with the autopilot, and the dangers of sailing the yacht near its limits downwind when, even fully crewed, the utmost teamwork and concentration were always needed to avoid breaking something.

I abandoned my effort to pass to the west of Cape Verdes and made a course to pass close to the east coast of Ilha de Sao Nicolau, one of

Trimming the headsail and examining the shape of the new sails during trials in the Solent. We only had six weeks to get the whole show on the water.

Above, adjusting the starboard autopilot control on the main cockpit control unit. Below, the autopilot heavy duty rams and motors linked directly on to the steering quadrant. Only one of the rams was driving the steering at any one time.

To keep *Group 4* moving single-handed I had to be all over the boat: adjusting the leech line on the staysail, above; below left, working at the deckplate just aft of the mast where all the mainsail reefing controls are situated; and trimming the staysail from the cockpit, below right.

Preparing for departure: above left, plastic crates in lieu of crew. There were in all thirty-eight red storage boxes of food, spares and stores. The yellow water-tight containers were used to transfer stills and video film at various rendezvous. Above right, the single sideband radio was one of my lifelines to the rest of the world. Below, the Chairman of Group 4, Jørgen Philip-Sørensen, encourages me to take on board a suspiciously weighty Christmas present from Chay.

Above, leaving Southampton on 21st November 1993, escorted by Challenge yachts, *Heath Insured* and *British Steel II,* and a host of wellwishers. Below, surfing past the mountainous west coast of Gran Canaria.

Above 30 knots of breeze a poled out yankee was just as efficient as a spinnaker, as demonstrated in this picture taken from *Craftsman's Art* at our Canaries rendezvous.

Below deck in my doghouse bunk or the galley gives no idea of the fact that all hell might be breaking loose above.

Turn right at Cape Horn. Above, the notorious graveyard of sail lies ahead with, below, the full might of the Southern Ocean beyond.

the central islands in the group. To pass to the west meant sailing dead downwind, which is highly inefficient. The sails simply become barn doors pushing the boat forward, rather than acting as efficient aerodynamic shapes. The result of not sailing directly downwind is to give the yacht an extra 2–3 knots of speed which made a course through the islands faster, despite the risk of more disturbed air in their lee. As I had observed off the Canaries, the disturbance created by islands in the otherwise steady flow of the trade winds can extend as far as 500 nautical miles downwind of an island and it is vital to take such considerations into account for a fast passage, whether racing or cruising.

In my mind's eye Chay, who had started a month earlier, was still far ahead of me. But I was catching him fast and had already reduced the deficit by over ten days. I would compare his progress of twenty-two years before against my own on a day to day basis. In this way I was effectively racing and this helped to provide the motivation to change sails, gybe and generally work the yacht in the most efficient way for as far as was possible twenty-four hours a day.

Although I had no real hope of matching *Group 4*'s time of the previous year, I was surprised to find that I was actually ahead of many of the Challenge yachts' times. I had picked up the trade winds earlier and kept them longer and the encouragement that this gave me was very rewarding, even if it was a slightly unfair comparison.

I spoke to Steve Moore at Autohelm and with his help soon had both autopilots fully functional again. Many of these early problems were just a lack of familiarity with the systems. The cutting out was cured by permanently fitting the two full function hand-held remotes. The one sited below enabled me to alter course while in my doghouse bunk and there was another at the mast which I used when I needed to reef or make adjustments to the variety of sail controls which were jammed off at the deck plate just behind the mast. These hand-held units had to have a little electronic handshake every once in a while. If one didn't get an answer, it would assume the worst and shut the whole system off. This caused the occasional upset but in general it was more an annoyance than a serious problem. A short sharp beeping tone would warn me of a cut-out and I was becoming much quicker in responding to the various different alarms I had set up.

Windshift, low boat speed, off course and time alarms were constantly going off and in many ways I felt that my performance would be directly related to both my tolerance and early response to these alarms.

I was still playing with the calibration and produced a list of optimum settings for different wind and sea conditions. This both conserved the pilots and the power needed to run them. I was amazed just how well they coped with the yacht, even downwind in heavy air. Helmsmen on the Challenge Race found these conditions tiring as the thirty-eight-ton Challenge yachts dislike being over-powered downwind, but the unrelenting concentration of the computer would make up for any lack of co-ordination or knowledge of the sea state.

The trend of 20-knot plus trade winds continued, but the knowledge that the doldrums could stop a yacht for many days encouraged me to pull in a constant stream of weatherfaxes from stations around the world. I could tune the single sideband radio (SSB) to one of the many stations in the Admiralty lists and, linking the headphone's output in to a laptop IBM PC equipped with fax software, I could obtain up to date information hour by hour. This sounds straightforward but a fault in the software meant I could only store one fax at a time and many hours could be spent trying to locate the best station and adjust the parameters to get the best picture.

On 7th December, seventeen days out from Southampton, I closed on Fogo and Brava, the most southerly islands of the Cape Verdes. *Group 4* was creaming along at over 11 knots. I helmed for long periods during the day, trying to hang on to the spinnaker and push west until 0430, then, dog tired, I changed down to a poled out yankee and got some rest.

When I woke at 0700 the last visible land until Brazil had gone.

3

Driving Hard
(Day 18 – Day 34)

Day eighteen was a day for dolphins. As I put up the spinnaker, I noticed that one of the battens had become detached from the cars which run up and down the back of the mast. Bringing the sail down, I spent several hours re-fixing it and tightening the others and generally checking the whole sail over again. Whilst tackling the mainsail I noticed the dolphins rounding up tuna a half mile or so from the boat. A few came over, but with the yacht not moving that well with the main down, they were soon bored and rushed off back to their fishing. Moments later I spotted a large whale's back fin as it dived just ahead and flying fish scattered out to the side of the boat. Of course I gave up work and went to grab the cameras but by the time I was back on deck . . . nothing. Sea life had been scarce so far. I remembered far more whale and dolphin sightings during the Challenge Race, when a shout from on deck would bring all the crew up to have a look. On my own, these beautiful aquatic mammals became a reassurance of the existence of other life, even in the most hostile places.

I baked a batch of bread to go with the last of the fresh food. Don and David had done a marvellous job and their checklist system was proving efficient and simple. Shortly, I would start using the sixteen basic varieties of long-life foods, so I relished the last of the fresh vegetables and meat. With Cape Verde behind I felt far happier. It was now a clear run down to the Horn, with the doldrums less than 300 miles ahead.

The next few days were wonderful and *Group 4* continued her charge south under spinnaker. Flying fish scattered the decks each morning and the only incident to interrupt the perfect sailing conditions was a split fuel line which filled the bilges with evil-smelling diesel – the one thing guaranteed to make me sea sick. To make matters worse, the hot weather made the fuel expand in the tanks, forcing neat diesel out through the breather pipes and making the decks as slippery as a skating rink. To cure the problem meant rigging a temporary pipe to a hand pump and pumping the excess into another tank.

Both autopilots were now sticking from time to time, not allowing me to turn the helm, even when the unit was on standby, so the club hammer now lived next to the rams. If I needed to take control, I developed a technique of steering with my foot whilst I gave the tiller bar a sharp bash with the hammer – not the most sophisticated way to treat state-of-the-art electronics, but the rams seemed very beefy and able to withstand the knocks. The cause of the sticking valves was becoming clearer – the electrical coils which operated them were supposed to be capable of being used continuously, but it seemed that they were, in fact, slowly breaking down. I had two spares on board but at the current rate of performance, they were not going to see me the distance.

By day 20 the doldrums began to make themselves felt. I was kept awake by lightning storms, and I waited for squalls which never seemed to come. Still the lightning was impressive, sometimes coming right down and striking the sea though, strangely, with no associated thunder clap. It was overcast and I was busy dodging rain clouds which can change the wind conditions in seconds. The wind under them either died completely or increased and shifted, forcing unnecessary sail changes. The variety of clouds that normally would never be seen together was incredible, layer upon layer from the alto-stratus to low level cumulus, with solid angled bands of tropical rain beneath them.

One such cloud passed overhead whilst I was talking with Chay on the SSB. He was in the middle of giving me doldrums advice when our conversation was cut short by the first bad squall. I was sailing with spinnaker, staysail and full mainsail – just about as much sail as *Group 4* can carry at one time, over 6,000 square feet. In seconds the wind rose to more than 30 knots and the boat lay down on her beam ends until I was able to get the spinnaker depowered. In the tropical downpour that followed I wrested the spinnaker down and, with two reefs in the mainsail, got underway again with fore and aft sails.

Twenty minutes later and the wind subsided and shifted back to the north-east direction it had been in before the squall and I was resetting the spinnaker, pouring with sweat in the unaccustomed heat.

It is easy to be fooled into believing that you have broken through the doldrums, only to find that the squalls, wind shifts and showers return with greater vengeance. But the following day I felt more optimistic. It was hard to believe that I had been held up for so little time. Just one squall and no period of calms seemed too easy to be true, but as the day went on and the wind steadily increased from the south-east, I became more and more certain that I had been let off easily. By far the the best indication was that the doldrums cloud had been replaced with more normal cloud formations. The forecast from Metroute in Bracknell confirmed it. The doldrums cloud had moved north and I was moving rapidly towards the south-east trades.

With the equator now only fifty miles to the south I looked forward to crossing into the southern hemisphere. The celebrations this time would be confined to a large Drambuie during happy hour before sunset, rather than the noisy and messy first-timers' party we had last year, but was a welcome datum point, and I was pleased to be several days ahead of my personal target.

I made a link call with my parents as I approached the equator. The whole family were having an early Christmas gathering for the benefit of the BBC team who were filming the call from their end, whilst I was videoing my end. We had a rather strung out conversation and I opened a couple of presents. The only member of the family not readily fooled by all this was my Gran who could neither hear me, nor see why we had to take liberties with the festivities. Thoughts of Christmas seemed especially strange as the temperature was now very oppressive and, being alone, I could not have felt more unChristmassy if I had tried. Still, it was good to hear all the family sounding so encouraging. It was as well I hadn't rewarded myself with too many slugs of Drambuie as, later that day, I found myself dangling from the mast on a block and tackle trying once again to repair the yankee leech line pocket which was by now beginning to disintegrate because of the continual flogging when reefing and unreefing.

Days end very abruptly in the tropics, and the nights were getting shorter. As it was getting dark on day 21 I could just see Sao Paulo and Sao Pedro, a pair of rocks, not big enough to be called islands, jutting up from 4,000 metres of water – an Everest amongst the undersea mountain range of the Mid-Atlantic Ridge. These rocks have huge populations of sea birds and are white with guano. One of the bonuses of ocean sailing is the opportunities to see at first-hand rare sights like this.

The following day when the sun came up I was wondering what I was going to do with the daylight hours. *Group 4*, as usual, provided the answers. Whilst putting a reef in the mainsail, one of the bungy cords that holds the reefing block snapped, and one of the jammer handles at the base of the mast broke off, when a line was caught around it during the reef. The jammer had to be drilled out. Then, using a 10 mm machine screw as an improvised tap, I cut a new thread. The new handle could be screwed in with epoxy resin to make sure it stayed put.

The broken bungy cord meant suspending myself out at the end of the boom and stitching a new one on. *Group 4* was punching along at 9 knots on a close reach, so this was an exciting operation. With this done, I looked at my watch and realised that there was only another two hours of light left. Everything takes so much longer on your own.

Occasionally I would set the watermaker to produce water enough for a shower, which always raised my spirits. I wasn't sleeping very well, the heat and humidity were just too much and a strained back from the continual heavy deckwork made finding a comfortable position difficult. The list of minor injuries was rising, too. Cuts on my hands were not healing because of constant immersion in salt water and both palms were calloused or raw from the continual spinnaker work. I spilt a molar tooth on a homemade cookie and, despite repeated attempts at repairing it with a tooth repair kit, it was starting to get tender and sore. I realised that I needed to become far more self-protective than I had been so far. Do-it-yourself dentistry may sound an ambitious way to start doing this. In fact it was a last minute gift from my uncle who came down to visit the boat proffering a tiny cardboard box which he had obviously had in his bathroom cabinet for some years. It contained little matchstick-size rods of clove-impregnated amalgam which you were supposed to melt and wipe into the tooth. I wasn't having much success.

Metroute at Bracknell were proving more useful, providing me with seventy-two-hour forecasts based in part on observations I sent back myself. It's a good service, and had been accurate in the North Atlantic. The forecasts were generally reliable but could be totally off the mark from time to time. On one occasion I was perplexed by a forecast for 'Gentle, moderate or strong winds', which pretty much covered all the options.

In the event I was experiencing strong south-easterlies, fast reaching winds which helped *Group 4* down towards the South American coast, while clear skies gave me some wonderful night sailing with bright bioluminescence, stars, shooting stars and even on one occasion a meteorite which briefly lit the sea for miles around.

With land now about a hundred miles away to starboard, I waited for the wind to veer and allow me to set spinnakers again. The south-easterlies turn down the coast and the prevailing wind on the coast at this time of year is north-east. I tried hoisting the spinnaker several times, but the wind was forcing my course far too close to the coast. Finally, by the evening, the spinnaker was up and with the pole set right forward and the wind slowly coming around, I could truly see the start of yet more wonderful downwind sailing in near perfect conditions.

I had said before departure that I intended to sail *Group 4* a gear down as far as the boat's possible and actual performance were concerned. In reality I hated doing this and on the whole it was proving unnecessary. I knew what the boat was capable of and found it difficult not to strive for this. The Southern Ocean might need a different approach but that remained to be seen and for the moment I was happiest driving the boat to near the limit. Of course, when things went wrong they were harder to deal with if the boat was over-pressed but, on the whole, I preferred to sail fast.

Changing charts for one with Cape Horn on it concentrated the mind on the fact that shortly I would be in the Southern Ocean. So I celebrated my success thus far with a small bottle of champagne and a chicken and pasta meal. Then I crashed out on the bench seat in the saloon, only to be woken by a flying fish which came in through the hatch and landed, thrashing wildly, at my feet. It gave me one hell of a fright before, now wide awake, I returned it to the sea.

Several ships passed close as I drew level with Recife and I stepped up my precautions for keeping a look out, setting radar and time alarms.

As the wind drew further aft, the temperature rose and I began to feel lethargic and tired. The decks were now so hot it was impossible to stand on them barefoot. Below, the Inmarsat terminal needed a small electric fan played on it, as the thermal cut-outs operated each day when the sun rose overhead. These were conditions it was impossible to escape from, fans simply moved the hot air around and I longed for the cooler weather. Any activity, on deck or below, had me pouring with sweat and cooking made the galley airless and unbearable.

The wind stubbornly refused to do what was expected and the spinnaker went up and down many times. I had mastered a technique for handling the spinnaker but it still took twenty to forty minutes from the decision to set the sail, and another thirty to get it down each time. In these frustrating conditions it was proving to be very hard work. Chay's book *The Impossible Voyage* had become an important reference in the navigation station so that I could check how we compared on the same day or in the same part of the ocean. Chay did not seem to use spinnakers, so when I had any opportunity to fly one I knew that my improved performance would be stripping miles away from his record. If he was having a bad day I would feel happier and if he was going well I would try harder.

Of course not every hour was spent working the boat, there was plenty of time for reading, writing and just sitting and watching the world go by. I would also use these times to do some filming. Three video cameras, two in waterproof housings, and three stills cameras kept me very busy at times. The organised film drops encouraged me to try to capture as much of what was going on as possible – whales, dolphins and sea birds were often around now, so the cameras were always kept at the ready and, with the promise of a forty-five minute BBC documentary, I knew I needed to shoot lots to get all they wanted. Of course some of the best photo-opportunities around the boat are when things go wrong on deck when it's impossible to film properly. But I was determined to do my best. I filmed myself washing up and pumping the bilges, I even filmed myself in the shower doing a strip-tease for the benefit of the camera, and then spent an awkward couple of minutes as I tried to work out how to cover up my essentials before coming out to switch the thing off.

The hot weather did not let up, and I drank extraordinary quantities of water or Refresh, a vitamin C-enhanced powdered orange drink, to replace the hourly fluid loss. This was crucial, as prolonged bouts of work could have me feeling dizzy and sick if I did not drink enough. By the evening of the twenty-sixth day the wind began to drop out again and progress slowed. I couldn't wait to get down to the Horn. I had been receiving telexes full of encouragement or news on almost a daily basis. Radio contact had become more difficult now and the Inmarsat became the front line communication link with the shore. I always enjoyed receiving telexes and knowing that news of the Group 4 Global Challenge was spreading further afield. I even received telexes from the Falklands where a former pupil of Challenge training skipper Pete Goss had ended up. He had followed the British Steel Challenge Race and was now monitoring my progress, sending good wishes and a radio frequency to call him on when I got closer.

The boat was often followed by sea birds and sometimes they would use *Group 4* as a resting point before continuing on their way. On 17th December, day 27, a young gull appeared, first trying to alight on the wheel which was spinning from side to side. He then tried to find quieter perches and appeared all over the boat. The final indignity occurred when he settled on the jockey pole which jerked as the spinnaker collapsed and refilled, throwing the poor bird many feet into the air, at which point he disappeared westwards in disgust.

I awoke from a short sleep to find the spinnaker wrapped tightly round the forestay. Normally I would have had a spinnaker net up to prevent this, but with the new furling systems the original net no longer fitted properly, I had not yet had time to modify it, and in my opinion a poor-fitting net was worse than none at all. After twenty minutes trying to steer the wrap out, and pulling at it from every angle, it seemed that I was going to have to go up the forestay and try to unwind it. I went below, pulled on the climbing harness, and came back on deck, only to find that it had sorted itself out without my help.

The day became a succession of near-miss spinnaker disasters. A few hours later I took the sail down again to gybe the boat. I was a bit casual about pulling it clear of the rail and the next thing I knew the cloth was pulling itself over the bows and rapidly filling with water. Any moment now *Group 4* was going to sail right over the top of it. This is one of the nightmares with spinnakers, not only could you lose the sail, but the ensuing mess could leave cloth wrapped on the keel or the rudder.

Recalling a similar experience on the Challenge Race, I gave up the losing battle at the guard wire, as the cloth poured over the rail and under the boat. I ran to the bows and tripped the guy with a tripping spike, allowing the sail to spill the ballooning water and relieve the weight. This enabled me to pull the whole lot in and to my relief it needed only a small repair. The light spinnaker was still a beautiful sail, although it was now on its second trip round, and it would have been a shame to lose it so early on.

In the afternoon I sailed close by a fishing boat on the outer banks of the Abrolhos Islands, 400 miles north of Rio. From a distance it looked very much like one we found stranded near Dakar earlier in the year. Fortunately, these men were in no danger and waved with enthusiasm rather than despair as *Group 4* surged past at 10 knots under the heavy spinnaker. Later I was able to make a link call to my parents. It was good to chat for a while but they had some bad news for me. I thought I had sold my flat when I left, but the buyer had pulled out. Trying to think about my domestic affairs from such a distance and in such a situation was near impossible. I thanked my lucky stars that my parents were in control and hoped that they could find another buyer soon. I was now reading Richard Bach's *Illusions*, the adventures of a reluctant Messiah, a gift from Challenge skipper Vivien Cherry. It was full of little gems of wisdom, the main theme being that you can do whatever you want to do! The right sort of encouraging reading as Christmas was approaching and I was becoming more isolated day by day with thoughts of home, family and friends growing seasonally stronger.

The brilliant downwind sailing ended the following day with the arrival of a 30-knot squall, rain, thunder and lightning. The squall passed within twenty minutes, but left a light head wind, which within an hour turned into a light tail wind. The weather felt cooler at last but progress was now difficult and slow. Squalls forced endless sail changes.

I was cheered to receive a telex from Alan Wynne Thomas and Merfyn Owen, two good friends who were sailing the 60-foot ultralight displacement boat *Cardiff Discovery* across the Southern Pacific from Hobart. Merfyn had designed my own 40-foot trimaran *Spirit of England* and I had sailed across the Atlantic with Alan a few years before – a very rough passage with five storms, but we had had a great time despite the weather. Alan is one of the hardest driving sailors I have ever met. He was forced to retire from the Vendée Globe Challenge (the French-organised eastabout solo race) when he was thrown from his bunk by a big wave and broke six ribs. He still managed to sail his yacht thousands of miles in a shocking physical condition, arriving in Hobart in January 1993 whilst the Challenge fleet was there. Now recovered, he was delivering *Cardiff Discovery* to the USA and a new owner. We set up a communications schedule and joked about the unlikely prospect of meeting at Cape Horn at Christmas.

In my log I began to consider fuel consumption as a potential long-term problem. So far the small diesel generator seemed very economical. I ran it once a day for four to eight hours, depending on the state of the batteries. So far I had only used a half of one tank, but inaccuracies in the measuring system and the fact that fuel would cross-feed from tank to tank through the tank breather was to make checking a problem. In the Southern Ocean I expected fuel consumption to increase as the heaters and radar (for icebergs) would be running most of the time. I was already concerned that the little generator would suffer from the continual heeling and pounding in the Southern Ocean.

At 0420 on the morning of 20th December I was startled into action by a loud crash. The whole boat shook from end to end as the spinnaker collapsed, backed and then wrapped around the forestay in 25 knots of wind. I had left the starboard autopilot on windvane, which enables the pilot to maintain the same wind angle, following all the slight wind shifts and alerting me of major direction shifts. The pilot was dead. The wrapped spinnaker came clear easily and, with the port pilot working, I began the long job of finding the fault in the starboard one. Because of their modular construction, fault-finding in autopilot components is fairly straightforward. The hardest task is when the fault is in the hundred of wiring connections. This time the pilots own built-in fault-finding system identified the problem area and the basic wiring diagrams which the installers and Autohelm had made up proved invaluable. After substituting several components, I eventually traced the fault to a dry solder joint on the port/starboard pilots switch in the nav. station. I hoped this would be the source of various intermittent faults I had had over the past few weeks. My little circuit tester proved its worth. Unfortunately, I still tend to think of electricity as water moving through fire hoses. I am no electrician.

It had been a frustrating day but, with both pilots working again, I rewarded myself with a meal of tinned steak and a bottle of red wine. As the passage progressed I began to build up a sail change diagram which would eventually help me to find the best sail combinations for the wind speed direction and sea state whatever the conditions. When you're cold and tired a good sail change diagram can help in the decision-making process and ensure you are getting the best out of the boat.

1 Wind 0–14 kts full sail
2 Wind 13–15 kts reef 20% yankee
3 Wind 16–18 kts reef 1 mainsail
4 Wind 18–20 kts reef 30% yankee (move car position)
5 Wind 21–22 kts reef 2 mainsail
6 Wind 22–27 kts 60% yankee,
7 Wind 27–35 kts reef 3 mainsail, 80% yankee.
8 Wind 35–40 kts reef 3 mainsail, 80% staysail
9 Wind 40 kts plus 80% staysail

Potentially the furling system gave almost infinite options between 15 and 25 knots of wind. But I could not keep on changing sail plans every five minutes and I needed to settle on a structured system. One of the biggest problems was that each change in the size of the yankee required the genoa car positions (sheet lead) to be moved either fore or aft. This plan meant that only one car position change was needed (at 18 knots), thereby saving both labour and wear on the sails which were by now showing small signs of abuse due to damage from flogging during changes.

My upwind sail change diagram was completed when I met a full gale on the nose on day 31. By the early hours of the next morning I was too exhausted to crawl into my bunk and simply slept where I had sunk on to the bench seat in the main saloon. When I woke the pilot had kicked into standby again because the mast remote unit could not take the solid water that had been breaking over the boat all night. Looking at the plotter on the GPS I could see that, in 35 knots of wind, *Group 4* had still managed to keep a remarkably good track since the cut-out, which meant the sail plan was obviously right for the boat to balance so well. By now the seas were really quite big and regularly breaking right over us, on one occasion taking one of the forward deck dorade ventilators overboard. Conditions were becoming quite severe. I was in for an interesting Christmas.

However, even with *Group 4* at thirty-five degrees of heel and crashing to windward, she was still steady enough for me to do some fiddly soldering when the radio handset stopped working. Meanwhile fresh bread was rising in strange contorted shapes in the oven which was not gimballed. *Group 4*'s saloon and galley remained both comfortable and usable in all conditions, a testimony to the designers. It was curious to see my track on the chart exactly matched our Challenge track on leaving Rio. The wind steadily lifted me round on to the course and with the prospect of some fast reaching past Florianopolis in Brazil I was reminded of the dilemma we had faced on the Challenge Race just twelve months before. Just a few days out of Rio de Janeiro our hopes of taking the lead were shattered in similar conditions when the forestay bottlescrew broke. I had to make a quick decision. I elected to head for Florianopolis whilst Group 4 hurriedly couriered a replacement part out to us. Later bottlescrews were to fail on many of the other yachts. But after forty-eight hours out of the race repairing this and the sails damaged in the failure we only caught the main fleet again in the Southern Pacific Ocean. Tomorrow I would be past the latitude of Florianopolis. This time a similar equipment failure would be a disaster if I was to take Chay's record.

The wind eased and backed round to the north-east, allowing the spinnaker to fly just before sunset. The large swells from the south left behind by the gale caused a very stressful motion as the boat sailed fast into each head sea, dropping into the trough behind, and momentarily allowing the spinnaker to part collapse and refill, shaking rig and sail violently each time. The whole effect was unnerving, uncomfortable and wearing.

The quieter sailing during the day allowed me to deal with one or two small jobs left behind by the wind of the past forty-eight hours. Trying to keep track of small bits of chafe on things like the running rig is always big job on a yacht of *Group 4's* size. Sailing solo, I often ran out of winches on the loaded up side of the boat. To overcome this I cross-winched, leading lines from the loaded side to the unloaded side. The raised coamings in the cockpit were a bad obstruction to this and chafed lines were the result. Flush-decked racing yachts have certain redeeming features.

Christmas Eve was a bright clear day with 30 knots of wind from the north-east. Messages piled in on the telex from friends and supporters sending their best wishes. I hope they realised just how much each message was appreciated. It spurred me on at a time when I was beginning to feel alone and missed the emotional and physical support of a crew. It seemed that nobody believed that I hadn't already delved into the multitude of Christmas presents. The one that had really tempted me was Chay's parcel. This was so big I wondered if it was full of bricks to slow *Group 4* down. But I had resisted all temptation. The days were stripping from the record and I was still well ahead of even my most optimistic planning. So Christmas Eve was business as usual, my only concession to the festivities a few decorations, and endless carols on the CD player piping through the deck speakers as I battled with the second reef, wearing the obligatory Santa hat. First thing in the morning was an interview with Radio Berks, followed by a special luxury, a pre-Christmas shower with hot water!

By now it was much cooler. Thermal clothing had again become the standard rig and great wandering albatrosses followed the boat toward their home in the wild air streams of the southern latitudes. A year ago we had sighted our first huge icebergs here off the South American coast. Icebergs were one of my major concerns in planning a route across the Southern Ocean. Fully crewed, a look out can be maintained, but alone I needed to plan to try to avoid the largest concentrations of ice, as the most dangerous bergs are not the huge tabular ones which would be visible on the radar or to the naked eye. It's the misleadingly named bergy bits or growlers that are the real worry. These are chunks the size of a house which only protrude one to five metres above the surface, but still have a lethal nine-tenths of their bulk lurking below. These are difficult, if not impossible, to see in rough conditions and are common around bigger bergs.

I thought a great deal about the risks of the Southern Ocean. Indeed, it was becoming an unhealthy preoccupation. But I knew the only thing to do was to press on day by day and actually get down there, and find out how to cope. I prayed that the Horn itself would be in a good mood. I was convinced we had all got past too easily last year – the Horn could be a terrible place to be battle around alone.

4

Turn Right at the Horn
(Day 35 – Day 45)

Christmas Day (day 35) began with a full gale blowing from the north-west after a very rough night's sailing, with steep waves dropping into the cockpit. Just about every sail went up and down as the wind shifted through west to east and I fell fast asleep during the afternoon, tired after the long night. When I woke, the wind had dropped right out, *Group 4* was trimmed for a beat, but the gentle wind from the east was more suited to the spinnaker. The effects of a good Christmas dinner and no sleep during the previous night had slowed me down.

I talked to family and friends on the radio, and afterwards linked up with various TV and radio stations. The reception was good and I even spoke to my parents who were in Cyprus. Radio communication was becoming more sporadic as I moved farther and farther south, so I took full advantage of periods of good reception. Between sail changes, I opened presents, not all at once but saving some for better conditions. There were many imaginative and thoughtful gifts designed to keep a mind occupied and Chay's huge parcel was not brick-filled after all. It was full of infuriating puzzle books and a tinned (inflatable) gold fish.

This was not the only inflatable pet – Griselda the life-size inflatable doll entered my life. I had a some fun filming her propped up in strange places whilst I was trying my best to give straight commentary to the onboard camera with Griselda peeping winsomely out of a cabin or hatchway in the background. Later I went on deck to do a sail change. When I came below I frightened myself to death as I turned into the saloon. I had forgotten I had left Griselda swinging from the ceiling. She was immediately deflated and returned to her box, my heart still pounding from the shock of seeing another body, even an inflatable one, on board.

Christmas dinner comprised chicken tikka and rice with Christmas pud and a brandy chaser. After dinner, with carols still playing on the stereo, I watched a tape of Christmas messages made up by Sumo and Martin on the day I left Southampton. This got me laughing and so relaxed that I had another brandy chaser.

Christmas was quite a landmark on the voyage. I had now sailed almost 7,000 miles and was heading towards a second New Year at sea on *Group 4*, again near Cape Horn. Three gales had tested all the systems very fully and, despite the problems, I felt confident that things were going as well as I could ever have expected.

The new sails, which had already done more miles than most cruising yachts' sails would ever do, still looked fresh from the sail loft. The generator now had a water leak which I could not cure. I prayed it would be okay. The autopilots seemed to have settled down, though I had eventually been forced to disconnect both the full function remotes, which allowed me to steer from the mast and below, as these were still causing a lot of minor compatibility problems.

I had spent the first thirty-five days preoccupied with the practical side of running the boat alone. Now I was just coming to terms with being alone for so long. My moods began to change with fearful rapidity but, rather than descend into a mire of introspection, I tried to refocus my attention towards the boat's performance. If at any time I failed to do something towards maximising this I would feel guilty and depressed until I had done something to compensate.

I could seldom sit for long with the wrong sails up, which as far as I'm concerned represents the worst effect of a lack of motivation aboard a boat. To safeguard myself from the danger of this steady downwards spiral, I began setting increasingly testing personal targets for myself, at first weekly, then daily, and eventually during each sail change, trying to stay motivated and keep things moving at all costs. That way I could see myself achieving success in smaller, more frequent, goals than the whole, and avoid the reefs of soul-searching.

On Boxing Day at last we had some smoother, gentler sailing with the lightweight MPG up. I opened more presents, and took advantage of the silky weather to catch up on some maintenance. I cleaned out the bilges, emptied the sump tank, did some washing, replaced valves on the derv transfer pump, refitted two locker doors (which had flown off during the Christmas Eve gale), took two extra turns on the furling drum, tightened the feeder arms, and transferred part of my canned fuel supply to the main tanks. Knowing everything I did was contributing to onward progress made it much less of a chore, in fact very satisfying. When I had done I made myself some fresh coffee and as I had just baked some fresh bread, the boat smelt like a French patisserie.

A gale from the west was forecast, adding to the tenseness of my approach to the Horn. Progress had slowed as the weather was by now either fickle or blowing a gale from the south-west. I was still heading to pass through Le Maire Strait between Staten Island and Tierra del Fuego, but the forecast was not looking good. The Falklands Current which flows north from the Horn was really very strong, several knots, despite my having been pushed towards the shallower, slower moving streams on the continental shelf. That evening the first of a series of depressions from the west moved in. The MPG was soon replaced by a reefed mainsail and the staysail, and I went below again cold and soaked. The wind continued to freshen all next day, and the sky looked heavy and threatening. The barometer was falling fast. The wind shifted to the south, allowing me to make some more progress inshore. Then it shifted suddenly during the night, quickly rising with gusts of 40 knots or more. It was very cold now, and the Southern Ocean beckoned.

I had resigned myself to using the main and staysail alone from 24 knots upwards, part reefing the headsail at 32 knots. It was going to be a severe test for the poor staysail and the inner forestay furling gear. In severe weather I firmly believe that it is safer to keep sailing, rather than lying ahull or running before and towing warps, as many of the old school prefer. I have tried these methods with some success, but on smaller, lighter yachts and multihulls. *Group 4* can keep going through most conditions, but to do it right, there must be enough power in the sail plan to climb the next wave. However well the boat keeps sailing, there are going to be moments, which a solo sailor particularly dreads, when he proves that flesh and blood are less resilient than steel. For me one of these was coming up.

As the wind eased, I was starting to shake out more sail and, whilst trying to take more turns of the sheet on the winch, the sheet was ripped from me by a gust, pulling my hands into the winch and self-tailer. There was blood all over the place. I felt distinctly sick as I looked at my left hand, the index and middle finger badly gashed through my leather sailing glove. When I got below and cleaned up, the damage didn't look so bad, only two deep cuts and some grazes, and my little finger had swollen so quickly I needed to cut the glove stitching to get it off. I realised the bone was either chipped or fractured, as it is swelled quickly and felt immobile. I strapped the finger to the one next to it and cleaned and dressed the wounds as best I could, adding this to the already impressive series of cuts and grazes I had accumulated since the start, for when continually immersed in salt water the simplest cuts refuse to heal properly and become pus-filled and sore.

With the forecast for more gales, I now looked anxiously for a slot to pass through Le Maire Strait. Rounding Staten Island would add an extra hundred nautical miles of sailing and I would arrive in the Southern Ocean sixty nautical miles to leeward of the prevailing westerlies. This would mean more time in the shallow water south of the Horn, the most infamous place on earth for sailing vessels. The following day was bright and clear, the wind shifting between south-west and west. But the Falklands were just sixty miles to port and it was proving impossible to stay on my favoured tack without heading straight on to the islands. I tacked and pushed west towards shallower water and some relief from the current. The forecast was still indicating strong weather for seventy-two hours and the whole plan of passing through the Strait was beginning to look dodgy.

In a brief respite I hove to with the intention of going to the top of the mast. The Windex had broken off during the last strong weather and, more importantly, I was concerned that the inner forestay bottlescrew (located at the top of the stay) had broken its monel metal seizing wires and this vital mast supporting stay was loosening. But about five feet off the deck I realised the impossibility of the situation. My hand throbbed with pain and blood poured through the dressings each time I tried to heave myself aloft. With the binoculars I inspected the bottlescrew from the deck and found that, although one part of the wire had fallen off, the screw was still held by a second band of wire. I fixed the spare Windex to the aerial mast on the stern as the safest compromise on that front and pressed on.

Sails, decks and many of the white melamine surfaces below were streaked with blood. Mine! The whole character of the passage had changed for the worse. Everything for the next few weeks was to prove harder as I tried to protect the injured hand from further damage. The cut on my index finger, which ran through the nail and the exposed quick, stung viciously on each immersion in salt water. I took to wearing a rubber glove. I began to get the most vivid dreams. In one I dreamt that I had finished the Global Challenge. All my friends were plying me with questions whilst I sipped a cool beer in the familiar surroundings of the bar overlooking the marina at Southampton and *Group 4*, looking good as new, was on the exhibition pontoon in the bright sunshine. Questions were being asked left and right, many of which I couldn't answer. I knew I was in a dream, and that I had only sailed as far as Cape Horn, but it didn't seem to matter. It was a good dream, so I didn't spoil it . . .

I woke quickly to the sound of rushing water above my head. Still in a haze, I pulled the foulies on and scrabbled on deck. The starboard pilot was playing up again, the motor was running but the wheel was not turning. With the boat off course we had been hit by a big wave. The bottom mainsail car universal joints had pulled clean out, the sail was bulging as the remaining joints were strained by the loss of lower ones, the whole lot was threatening to burst uncontrollably loose at any moment. I found myself five foot up the mast, soaking wet, repairing the car, still dreaming of better times.

This week was to become very testing, the number of breakages was growing and the weather seemed determined to stop me making it around the corner. Every mile had to be fought for. The breakages could be fixed in time or I could adapt the way I did things so as to do without an item damaged beyond repair. But it was frightening how quickly things had changed, from the carefree days of the trade winds. Working the yacht with one hand effectively useless or in agony had a terribly demoralising effect. Ahead was the toughest sail of my life and my physical state was rapidly deteriorating with each additional injury. The Southern Ocean is no place for failures, there is no back-up, no places to stop and fix or recuperate. Each time I reefed a sail I reminded myself that one slip would at best mean real problems, at worst certain death. Physically and mentally I was becoming exhausted, by all the hours spent nervously watching wind speeds or directions, looking for the time to reef or tack, asking myself should I or shouldn't I, endless questions, and I had not even rounded the corner. I conceded a limited defeat and eased back the pressure, knowing I needed time to mend if I was to make a success of the thousands of miles ahead.

As we came up to the New Year I was chatting with *Cardiff Discovery* on the SSB. We had established regular radio schedules as we closed with each other from different directions. Our tracks were clearly going to meet either at or very near to the Horn. The wind dropped out just as midnight arrived and, relishing the break, I cracked a bottle of whisky and toasted all the people who had made Global Challenge possible. As a mental exercise I tried to visualise each person in turn and toast each one independently – a good exercise which became increasingly difficult until finally I fell asleep where I sat.

The wind stayed light and on the nose on New Year's Day and huge rolling swells from a severe gale to the south prevented me from making good progress. But the fine, if crisp, weather allowed me to repair the starboard pilot. After a lot of crawling about with the circuit tester, I was able to trace the problem back to the bypass valve which controls the flow of hydraulic oil in the ram. On inspection it had really blown, the whole body had expanded and it was now impossible to separate the coil from the valve body. I fitted a replacement, my last but one, and hoped the problem was isolated to this one faulty component.

The pilot tiller bar, an enormous chunk of engineering, had started to work loose on the rudder stock head. I was amazed to see movement here, as I thought we had over-engineered this fitting by many time. I drove shims made with stainless steel washers down the gap at the side and, with all movement gone, I experienced no further problems. The loads on both the autopilot rams and the steering gear were tremendous – far in excess of those experienced by a yacht on a normal ocean passage. When *Group 4* pounded to windward in these steep seas, leaping from wave to wave, and dropping like a stone for many feet between them, the impact was transferred directly back through the entire steering system. I added a series of regular checks on this to the growing list of daily and weekly checks.

On the morning of 2nd January I came very close to a big Japanese factory ship. They had steered a parallel course all night, preventing me from getting much rest, but in the morning the ship started to close the distance as if to coming to have a look at me. To my horror it just seemed to keep coming. In the end, not wishing to be run down, I tacked and got clear. Then I went below and taught him some English words on the radio – they did not respond, not even in Japanese.

The weather reports all indicated that the wind would moderate and pick up again from the north, perfect for a passage through Le Maire Strait. Sure enough the wind moderated and was blowing largely from the west, shifting to south-west for twenty minutes every couple of hours. This was allowing me to make for the Strait most of the time, a saving of fifty miles or more on my route. But in the afternoon the wind rose suddenly and was soon blowing from the south-south-west at 35 knots. Some recalculation showed that it was going to be impossible for me to arrive at the Strait on a favourable tide. The tide through the Strait can exceed 6 knots. With a strong head wind and current I would simply not make it through. Even if I waited for a favourable tide, the seas would be fierce, with the strong winds blowing against the tidal flow. The risk of damaging something was just too high. So regretfully, I decided to sail the extra miles and pass round the eastern side of Staten Island, or Isla de los Estados. I hated being forced to do this. If you catch Le Maire Strait right, as we had the previous year, it can really slingshot you into the Southern Ocean.

The cold shadow of land now appeared ahead, the first true land I had seen since the Canaries and the most south-easterly tip of South America. The Admiralty Pilot advised that I remain ten miles to the east. The severity and unpredictability of the area ensured that on this occasion I would follow the Pilot's advice, however begrudgingly. On 3rd January the wind picked up and, sailing through the

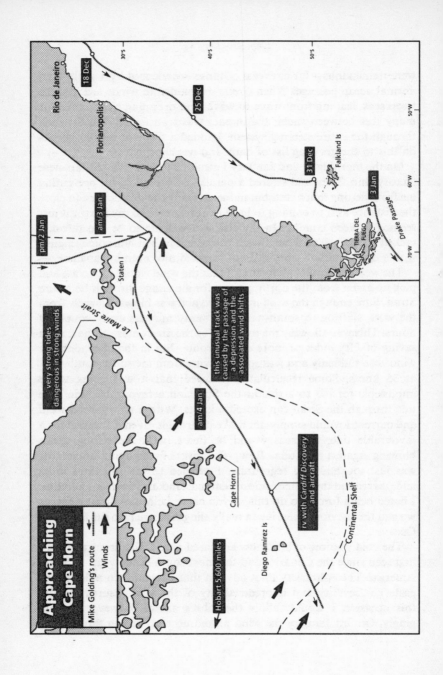

Approaching Cape Horn

Mike Golding's route

Winds

18 Dec
25 Dec
31 Dec
3 Jan

Rio de Janeiro
Florianopolis
Falkland Is
TIERRA DEL FUEGO
Drake Passage

pm/2 Jan
am/3 Jan
am/4 Jan

Staten I
Le Maire Strait

very strong tides
dangerous in strong winds

this unusual track was
caused by the passage of
a depression and the
associated wind shifts

rv with Cardiff Discovery
and aircraft

Cape Horn I
Diego Ramirez Is
Hobart 5,600 miles
Continental Shelf

30°S
40°S
50°S
50°W
60°W
70°W

water at 9–10 knots, *Group 4* struggled forward making only 5 knots over the ground, with the strong current setting north. The combination of the wind and tide made the sea very agitated with steep-sided standing waves, overfalls and tide rips. It quickly became very clear why many sailors had needed to retreat from the Horn. I kept a careful watch on the navigation. The current was dragging *Group 4* towards the rugged coastline and constant small course changes were needed to ensure we did not end up too close and overwhelmed in the tidal races on the east coast of Staten Island.

As *Group 4* met the full blast of the Southern Ocean Current nothing could be seen through the light mist that had descended, but the air was thick with the scent of heather from Tierra del Fuego. The sea and skies merged into a uniform greyness and the new coldness bit deeply.

When we passed through this area in the Challenge Race, it was a very different experience. Most of the yachts had light airs and *Group 4* was on a roll and catching the fleet after our disastrous bottlescrew failure. We had already passed two of the other yachts and now the weather helped us to close the gap on the main body of the fleet. We had arrived at the Strait at the perfect time and shot through at over 14 knots over the ground, arriving at the Horn only eight hours later. At the Horn we had picked up a north-east breeze and an hour later achieved 21 knots, surfing on a steep sea, the highest recorded speed by any yacht during the race.

Now the current eased as *Group 4* moved into the area. I continued to push south, then west, moving towards the tidal lee of Cape Horn itself. The forecasts, whether local or otherwise, were unreliable in this part of the world. I learned to trust barometer readings and cloud observations far more, though for longer range and more general weather changes, the weatherfaxes were still worth the significant time and effort to raise the appropriate stations. The wind dropped completely and for a time I furled the headsails to reduce the chafe from flogging and drifted on the huge swells with just the mainsail up and sheeted in hard amidships. The mist lifted and the south coast of Staten Island appeared to the north. A pod of large pilot whales surrounded the boat and the warm sun burned through the last remnants of haze changing the whole scene and bestowing on me one of those sights and sensations that are so rare but make ocean-sailing so addictive. Though I hated being becalmed here because I just wanted to head west and get away from the dangers of the Horn, it was wonderful to watch whales only feet away and in their natural environment.

Early the following morning, 4th January, a gentle breeze sprang up from the north-west, heralding the approach of a new weather system. *Group 4* passed only a few miles to the south of the jagged silhouette of Cape Horn as the sun, which at night here seemed just to dip below the horizon rather than set, angled up again, reflecting the whiteness of the snow-topped mountains of Tierra del Fuego. I was past the Horn and heading south-west, only Antarctica lay ahead.

The wind rose steadily and *Group 4* raced to get clear of the shallow-water shelf that makes this area so dangerous. Talking with Alan on *Cardiff Discovery*, it became increasingly certain that we would now pass close enough to make a rendezvous possible. We were both suitably staggered at the coincidence of meeting in such circumstances, and we sighted each other in the late afternoon, closing quickly. I hove to, effectively stopping and as they made their final approach, I rigged a heaving line to a watertight container filled with ready meals, some Scotch, champagne, chocolate and a Fireman Sam bubble bath for good measure, and heaved this mini-Christmas hamper across as they passed *Group 4*'s stern. The rules of the Global Challenge of course prevented them returning the seasonal compliment. With shouts in both directions and some hurried filming and photography, they rapidly receded into the clutter of steep waves towards the Horn. The whole rendezvous had taken just four minutes.

With *Group 4* sailing again I pressed her towards the relative safety of deeper water on a track passing south of Diego Ramirez, a cluster of islands to the south-west of the Horn. A Chilean aircraft carrying a film crew crackled a garbled message on the portable radio. They were approaching from the north, but with the weather closing in fast and low clouds hiding the top of the islands ahead, the chances of them finding *Group 4* decreased by the minute. Suddenly, in excited and heavily accented English, the pilot announced that he could see me. I rushed on deck and looked around but could not see or hear anything. He still claimed to see me and it was a few seconds before I realised what was happening. The pilot was closing on *Cardiff Discovery*. With the hand-held radio batteries fading fast I tried to tell him he was busy filming the wrong boat, but he would have none of it.

'Okay. I see you ahead. I see you. Over.'

'It's not me. Over.'

'But yes, I see you. Over.'

'No, you don't. Over.'

This inane conversation, rendered more ridiculous by the language barrier, was cut short by the batteries finally giving up. Meanwhile, heading east, Alan and Merfyn, I discovered later, were managing the farcical situation not much better. They had just begun to toast me in my champagne when they found themselves being buzzed by a Twin Otter. Guessing the mistake, they began pointing vigorously to the south-west, but the pilot in a frenzy of Chilean goodwill waved back. The more they gesticulated, the more enthusiastic he became. By this time I had plugged the radio into the charger below and waited for five frustrating minutes as the batteries charged sufficiently for me to have another try. Eventually, I got one garbled message to the pilot who finally seemed to understand as the batteries gave out again. Or maybe he had just got round to counting the number of figures leaping up and down aboard *Cardiff Discovery*.

Ten minutes later the Twin Otter, flying low beneath the cloud, appeared from the north. As if on cue dolphins played in the waves around the boat. I took the helm and with 10,000 miles of the loneliest most desolate ocean ahead, crashing south-west in a 67-foot yacht, I felt ten feet tall and grinned maniacally from ear to ear. I was on my way and surely nothing could stop me now.

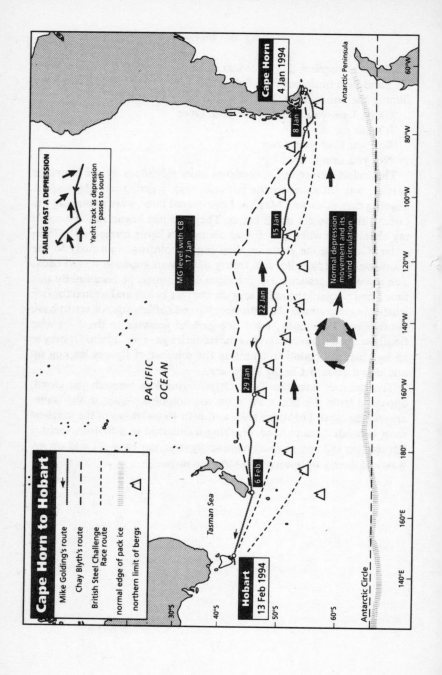

Cape Horn to Hobart

- Mike Golding's route
- Chay Blyth's route
- British Steel Challenge Race route
- normal edge of pack ice
- northern limit of bergs

Cape Horn 1994
4 Jan 1994

8 Jan

15 Jan

MG level with CB
17 Jan

22 Jan

29 Jan

6 Feb

Hobart
13 Feb 1994

PACIFIC OCEAN

Tasman Sea

Antarctic Peninsula

Antarctic Circle

SAILING PAST A DEPRESSION

Yacht track as depression passes to south

L

Normal depression movement and its wind circulation

60°W 80°W 100°W 120°W 140°W 160°W 180° 160°E 140°E

30°S 40°S 50°S 60°S

5

No Law, No God
(Day 46 – Day 54)

I felt exhausted after rounding the Horn. Sailing in such close proximity to land had forced me to stay alert for much of the time. As we cleared the continental shelf I was sleeping the sleep of the dead and woke only when the klaxon alarm sounded. I was due to radio link with Philip Sørensen and Chay who were hosting a press conference at the London Boat Show.

The wind continued to rise and soon became a full gale with seas to match. I went on deck to reef the main and furl the yankee and it was twenty minutes before I got below again. Then, I tried to reach Portishead on the radio, but I could not hear anything. I telexed to let them know I was calling on 22 khz. Twenty minutes later a thin crackly voice came through the speaker. Philip, then Chay, shouted their best wishes down the airwaves but reception was very poor and the difficulty heightened my sense of remoteness. I had been looking forward to the link up and felt annoyed with myself for not trying to establish it earlier in the day when reception might have been clearer.

The wind rose further, the passage of two clearly defined cold fronts produced regular 50-knot gusts. The frontal trough responsible extended for thousands of miles to the west and I could see from the weatherfax that I was heading into a prolonged period of bad weather. Already the seas had become huge and conditions were as rough as I had ever seen. In conditions like this the boat crashes over, often through the enormous seas which travel towards it at more than 40 mph. Each time a steep-sided wave hit, nearly forty tons of yacht would be left in mid-air, dropping like a stone into the trough with a devastating, bone-crushing slam at the bottom. Everything would become weightless for seconds before the shock produced on each impact. Keeping *Group 4* moving when conditions became this bad demanded supreme confidence in the yacht's design and construction. This was where my knowledge of the boat's capabilities started to pay off.

Each squall would find me sitting in the nav. station watching the wind instruments with a horrified look on my face and the feeling that the next gust could certainly break something. On deck waves swept over *Group 4* as though she wasn't there. Working on deck at night was frightening. I prayed for a wind shift to the south-west so I that could head further north. I was heading south-west on the favoured tack, closing with the ice and the ever-increasing risks of sailing in higher southern latitudes. The shortest route across the Southern Ocean between Cape Horn and New Zealand is to sail a composite great circle route. This means following a great circle as far south as is prudent before taking a westerly rhumb line route clear of heavy ice areas, and then finally a northerly great circle route on towards New Zealand. The farther south one sails in the Southern Ocean the faster the boat crosses the meridians of longitude as they converge towards the Pole. But as you go deeper south, the more unpredictable and violent the weather can become. I was already at 58° South, so there seemed little point in pushing my luck farther. I waited for a wind shift to allow me to get farther north.

The following day the gale blew with undiminished ferocity. The seas were of staggering proportions now. When the wind gusted over 50 knots the tops of the waves calved off, dropping on deck, and pressing *Group 4* down into the water with the momentary additional weight of tons of water. At last, on 6th January, the wind finally shifted west and I began to make some northing. We now met the seas head on, the sheared wave tops sent white cascading water, four foot deep, surging along the full length of the boat. I began to consider heaving to and waiting for better conditions, even with only a part furled staysail and no mainsail the boat crashed along and felt pressed in the most extreme gusts. I watched each gust with increasing anxiety, but minute by minute *Group 4* seemed to cope. In the Challenge Race we had always tried to press on, as the boat seemed less vulnerable when kept moving. But now I felt less inclined to do so. A problem on deck in these winds would be almost impossible to deal with single-handed. Just moving around on deck was dangerous, reducing me to crawling on hands and knees, even to get to and from the mast, let alone do anything when there. Nineteenth-century whalers used to say that beyond 40° South there is no law, beyond 50° South no God, and I was beginning to believe them. It was plain bad luck to be hit so hard so soon.

Pain from my injured left hand reached new levels. The skin had not had a chance to dry and the cuts had become sore, infected and pus-filled. Every time I handled sails or lines a continuous trail of watered down blood marked my progress round the decks. I pumped pain-killers down every few hours and felt woozy, detached and more tired than ever.

On 7th January the low pressure system responsible for the foul weather finally passed over ahead and the barometer began to rise again. The wind swung west, then south-west and at last I was able to tack on to port and make some more northing. During the night I made eighty miles of northing and was delighted next morning to find our latitude back up at 57° South. The wind started to ease and I tried to shake a reef out too early. Thirty knots of wind seemed like nothing after prolonged periods of 45 knots, but I needed to put the reef back in a few minutes later. However the wind did drop further which allowed me to work *Group 4* back through the various sail plans. By midday I carried full sail again and made slow progress through the enormous, wonderful seascape left by the storm-force winds. The sun came out, the sky cleared and the wind shifted south-west allowing me to lay the desired course for the first time since the Falklands. This spell gave me a chance for a much needed wash, time to dry some clothing and, after a good relaxed meal of prawn curry, I quickly began to feel a hundred per cent better. Memories of bad weather fade extraordinarily quickly.

I also took the opportunity to tackle some maintenance. First I serviced the generator, which had now done 300 hours, then I disassembled the steering wheel clutch to tighten the screws which held it on. Looking around the yacht for signs of real damage, I could find none. We had come through our first Southern Ocean storm virtually damage-free.

I was still trying to keep tabs on what was going on at home through the Inmarsat terminal and what I was hearing sometimes made me wonder if reliable communications were not a mixed blessing. I occasionally felt like ripping the terminal out and chucking the thing over the side in frustration. I had spent the best part of two years away from home, first on the Challenge Race and now this. My personal affairs had been left unattended for too long and I had been trying to sell both my home and yacht to simplify matters. Now both transactions appeared to have fallen through for the umpteenth time. I imagined all sorts of financial problems confronting me on my return. In reality my parents and friends were doing everything possible. But I made a conscious effort to avoid further communications on personal matters – it was too easy to become worked up about the wrong things. I felt I had enough problems within the confines of the boat and did not need to take any external worries on board.

The wind soon shifted back through west and began to increase from the north. A layer of high cloud moved in from the west, the first sign of the next system and more gales. Waiting for a gale to come is always far worse than actually dealing with it once it arrives. The weatherfax and forecasts from Metroute all indicated gales, but it came to nothing and I made good progress the following night, waking frequently to check the wind speed. A heavy mist descended, not fog but enough to merge sea and sky into a grey blur. Deckwork became extremely cold and damp and I began running the diesel heaters for most of the time, as everything below had become sodden with condensation.

The continuing quiet conditions gave me a chance to check how the stores were holding out. I was now approaching one third of the whole distance and needed to stocktake. Following Don and David's famous food checking system, I simply had to look up the required item and its location, then, like supermarket shopping, trot off to the right cabin and rummage through the storage boxes, pick out what I wanted, remembering to strike it off the inventory sheet.

An average meal could be prepared in just fifteen minutes by boiling a pack in water. If I was feeling more adventurous in the galley I might open a tin or bake some bread. All the food was almost too easy to cook. Eventually, I longed for fresh ingredients and a more flexible diet. I would have enjoyed more challenging things to cook. Some of the long-life food had become boring. Chicken tikka and rice started to taste just like beef stew and dumplings, all of them packed with preservatives. I believe it's almost inevitable on a very long passage, and I worried about getting the right balance of vitamins, roughage and calories. I would not always eat well when conditions were bad, choosing the easy food rather than a balanced selection. In the Southern Ocean a man can use as much as 6,000 calories just supplying the energy to fend off the cold and motion. Heavy deck-work adds to this figure and simply eating the right amount of food a day was proving difficult – even with my appetite.

Fuel and gas seemed to be lasting well. So far I had used only one bottle of gas, though in the sub-zero temperatures of the Southern Ocean I knew I would get less out of each bottle in the months ahead. As for fuel, I was still running on the first of five tanks. This made me suspicious that it had been siphoning from tank to tank when the boat was heeled. With no sight gauges I was forced to guess the levels remaining.

The next low pressure passed to the north of me and brought following easterly winds. The rapidity of wind direction changes made the hassle of setting up all the spinnaker gear very unattractive. I reached north-west on starboard gybe as the wind quickly changed from north-east through south-east and eventually settled in the south. Reluctantly, I reeved the spinnaker gear and, after a few hours of watching and waiting, I eventually hoisted the heavy spinnaker.

Forty-nine days at sea, and the favourable spell in the weather continued, allowing good progress and just the break I needed to allow my hands to heal. They were still very sore and calloused, but at last with the heaters on below they were able to dry up and the cuts began to skin over. My little finger stopped throbbing and the swelling reduced. I ran out of dressings and began to use sticky Dacron (for sail repairs) as plasters.

Finally, the wind dropped out completely, I wound everything in tight and lay down below. But the continual slatting of sails made sleep impossible and I got up to spend several cold hours trying to coax some miles with the MPG. Eventually what wind there was shifted east, then backed south. With the barometer reading 970 mb, I was passing directly underneath the low centre, the eye of the storm. It was a strange feeling to know that gales raged all around. The seas became highly confused, great spikes of water, rising up in standing waves, halted what little progress I could make with the sails still slatting from side to side. As soon as the wind stopped shifting it began to build again. Twenty minutes later there was over 25 knots and, skipping the first reef, I snugged *Group 4* down for the next heavy blow.

At first light a full gale was blowing again, as we charged along down the course line, taking my track on the chart through longitude 90° West. Each line of longitude had become a milestone worthy of celebration. Radio communication with Portishead was by now near impossible and I made my first clear link with Sydney Radio, another welcome sign of progress, for updating my plot on the chart, which spanned from South America to New Zealand, had become depressing. Each plot represented so little overall progress, I put the charts away in the chart table and from here onwards updated my position only once every few days.

The constantly changing weather kept me busy with sail changes but with no change in the general situation from day to day, boredom became a problem. I read a great deal. Ranulph Fiennes' autobiography was the current book. I normally hate autobiography, but he has led such an extraordinary life. Some of his nastier experiences put all of my problems into perspective. Day 50 felt as though we were sailing through glue. All day the wind blew from either side of my intended course and a strong current slowed us to a crawl, as I tacked back and forth in an attempt to make some headway. The tacking and my attempts at driving *Group 4* hard opened the leech line pocket on the yankee again, despite my having stitched it up before the Canaries. Now the block hung out and threatened to smash and chafe through the line or, worse, tear the staysail during a tack. For the time being I furled the sail and continued under main and staysail, shaking a reef to make up some of the lost power.

Down below was a nightmare. The tacking back and forth in bad weather had caused cupboards to burst open, ripped the door hinges off and sent the contents all over the saloon and galley floors, most things ending piled upon the port tack.

On a happier note I received a telex from Kim Fitzsimmons of BT and was delighted to hear that *Nuclear Electric*'s John Chittenden was to receive the Yachtsman of the Year Award. On the Challenge Race he had become the skippers' skipper and was a most worthy recipient. Indeed, he was one of the first people I approached for advice after formulating the Global Challenge, because I knew how valuable his reaction would be.

Although I had sailed several degrees north, the temperature was falling, by first light the cockpit had a thin layer of ice on it, and I had changed into the highest performance Henri Lloyd thermal gear. Only my hands suffered, not so much from the injuries, but from the excruciating pain of the warm-ups after prolonged deckwork. I started doing leg exercises, as I was beginning to get cramps in my feet from not walking enough. I felt, and I'm sure looked, comical, wedged on my back into a spot in the companionway, with the boat at thirty degrees, pedalling like fury or, worse, jogging on the spot at thirty degrees to the surrounding furniture. But I wanted to be able to walk off the boat at the end. By the evening the frustrating day's progress needed exorcising with a few beers and a good sleep.

My entries in the navigation log for the 10th, 11th and 12th January were simply 'Damn', 'Blast', and 'Hell', or words to that effect, scrawled over each page. It was depressing to see how slow progress was, despite the fresh breeze. It had been a mistake to marry the West Pacific chart, with South America on it, to the East Pacific chart with New Zealand on it. I thought it would be interesting to see how far I had come, but I had scarcely scratched the distance. It just seemed to be going on for ever. I tried everything, but progress was nowhere near what I had hoped to achieve, based on our Challenge Race performance. The biggest single slowing factor was the need to remove the whole yankee when the wind reached 24 knots and I could feel my day to day averages falling back. Stronger currents than I had expected from the routing charts also chipped away at my hard fought for progress. I lost count of the number of tacks I put *Group 4* through and I seemed to be constantly reefing or un-reefing. I could not recall experiencing such an unremitting period of fruitless beating before.

Looking in the mirror, I hardly recognised myself. Bearded and drawn, with grey bags under my eyes, I looked far worse than I actually felt. After a wash and shave I changed into a new set of thermals and dried my Henri Lloyd foulies in the engine room. Hours later everything was wet again but I felt better for having made the effort. It is far too easy to allow personal standards to slip out of control on a long solitary voyage.

I had chosen to try to stay on the rhumb line (a straight line on the chart). The option of heading north seemed attractive but the weatherfaxes showed that the weather directly to the north of me was little better. The roaring forties and screaming fifties were living up to their reputation and showed an uninterrupted flow of strong westerlies all the way across to New Zealand. The individual weather systems tracked south-east at 40 knots or more, crossing well south of my track where I had no wish to go, deep into iceberg country. The reality is that sailing upwind does not allow much freedom of movement across the track. There needs to be good reason to deviate from sailing on the most favourable tack and the systems tracked across so quickly there were few occasions when I was able to manoeuvre *Group 4* into the perfect position in time to get the best out of each wind shift.

The biggest limiting factor this far south was a fear of getting in amongst ice. The bergs which break away from the Antarctic continent do so on a scale quite unknown in Arctic regions. In 1977 the Whitbread Race yacht, *Debenhams*, skippered by John Ridgway, tried to cut the corner to gain a mileage advantage on competitors. But he was forced to turn north for twenty-four hours when solid pack ice blocked his path at only 59° South. Sailing through ice regions with a full crew is one thing, but the risks to a single-hander are far greater because he is unable to maintain continuous visual look out, and has far less chance of sighting dangerous semi-submerged growlers in his path which won't in most cases show up on radar. In Arctic waters there is an international organisation which monitors and co-ordinates ice reports. No such equivalent exists for the southern oceans, and the main information comes from US satellites which provide reports on the position of the edge of the pack ice. As for the northern limit of icebergs, this is seasonal and also varies considerably from year to year. I was told it would be pretty clear above 63° South. But one knew one still had to look out for the stray growler or bergy bits which are so much more of a hazard than the huge tabular bergs we had seen the previous year. Careful watch of the weather and monitoring changes in sea water temperature were important.

The mist lifted and the sun came out the afternoon of the 12th and, although I was still struggling to make headway, conditions seemed far more pleasant. Reading Chay's book, I could see similar frustrations and experiences. I also saw that he was not far ahead of me now. Soon I would be overtaking him and, I hoped, pulling away – it was a great encouragement. Racing invisible yachts, whether Chay's or the Challenge fleet, had become the prime motivation for crawling out of a cosy sleeping bag in the middle of the night. It was certainly a better incentive than my inch by inch progress across the chart.

Frequently I would be woken by one of the many alarms, sounding a gentle beeping. If I ignored this, after twenty seconds the klaxon version would have me leaping to get into my thermals and foulies. Fire Service training served me well, helping me rig quickly and properly in multiple layers, safety harness, gloves and a hat before going on deck. More than half of the alarms would mean the boat was over-pressed. On deck biting winds, hail, snow or heavy spray would startle me into action and within moments I would be abusing muscles that just a few minutes before were relaxed in sleep.

A simple tack could involve fifteen minutes of hard grinding on overloaded winches. Steep waves swept the decks because of the excessive angle of heel. At night, working in the dim glow of the deck light, thoughts of the how-in-the-hell-did-I-get-here variety often crossed my mind, and I smiled at the seemingly ludicrous task I had set myself. Climbing back to the wheel in pitch dark, I would find the unlit buttons of the autopilot controls and adjust the yacht's course to feather the boat into the wind, releasing some of the excess wind pressure and easing the angle of heel. Waves would now break over the bows with increased ferocity as the yacht met the seas head on. Clipping on to the upwind jackstay, I would make my way forward to the white water crashing past the mast. This breaking water, often four foot deep, was responsible for many injuries on the Challenge, picking even the biggest men up and sweeping them many feet down to the leeward guard wires with just inches separating the safety of the boat from the Southern Ocean and certain death. I constantly reminded myself of this when working at the mast in these conditions, and crouched low to the deck. Crawling was wetter but at least I could not be knocked over so easily. The reefing process was usually straightforward, but carried out in the midst of a foaming, freezing turmoil of water, any one of a hundred things could go wrong if tiredness caused a mistake. Fortunately, now it had become an almost automatic procedure.

Making my way back to the cockpit, I would steer for a time, re-trimming the sails to balance the yacht before switching the pilot back on. Trimming the yacht correctly naturally increased the boat speed but, as importantly, it reduced the load on the pilot system, saving both power and wear.

Twenty minutes after emerging on deck I could head below again, with the satisfaction of knowing that the boat was now doing its best. I would peel off the damp layers and arrange them carefully to give them the best chance of drying out before the next alarm. Climbing back into my damp sleeping bag was like heaven. In minutes I would be back deep in the vivid dreamland special to offshore sailing. The next alarm could come in minutes or, if I was lucky, a couple of hours.

Sailing in the Southern Ocean often provided days and days of endless rounds of sail changes. When I was tired I found myself working in a trancelike state, moving slowly around the deck in a methodical routine way that helped to keep me safe, my mind often elsewhere. I began to think of the next person who would attempt the same record. Whilst I was here I was determined to do as much as I could to make his or her life more miserable than my own – the Global Challenge rules said nothing about being graceful or making the next challenger's job a pleasure cruise.

Eventually the wind eased, the sun came out, and seas moderated, although the unfavourable wind direction continued. I produced some hot fresh water and had an invigorating shower, changing the thermals I had first put on at the Falklands. The wind now played games with me, blowing from all round the compass. But at last I was able to make fair progress in the right direction. I crossed 110° West. Finally, I was able to put the chart with South America, and all the plots since Cape Horn, away into the chart table. I had crept on to the margin of the chart with New Zealand on the far left-hand side and I studied it as avidly as one would a freshly delivered morning paper.

6

The Longest Beat
(Day 55 – Day 72)

The morning of 14th January found me busily surrounding myself with enough little plastic containers for a teddy bears' picnic. I was servicing the winches. Cogs, springs and pawls were everywhere, soaking in their separate baths of diesel to remove old grease and salt. One of the primary winches had failed during the night, instantly releasing several tons of load as the sheet screamed off the winch drum. I had furled the sail and crawled forward to retrieve the sheet, re-reeving it back through a spare block attached with a Spectra strop to the failed winch and across the boat to the starboard primary winch. The failed winch had broken one of the brass alloy collets that held the drum in place and the pawls, grungy with salt crystals and old grease, were sticking. The central shaft had been burred by the force of the failure and needed filing down to allow the drum to be refitted. After fitting a few replacement parts, cleaning, greasing and servicing, it ran as smoothly as ever. I added winches to my ever growing cycle of weekly servicing and checks.

My fingers were now healing well, although the joints remained stiff and tender. I had become very self-protective, and would sooner see a sail flogging or steer in the wrong direction than put myself at risk of further injury. The hourly inconvenience and irritation from the hand injury had made life on board twice as uncomfortable as was necessary. I had learnt the hard way that I could not afford to risk further injuries. Baking bread had become a regular treat. In rough conditions, especially when the boat was heeled over heavily, the bread rose at

89

a slant and sometimes produced some very odd shapes, but it always tasted superb, and was now the freshest food I had aboard.

The sea smoothed out on the 15th, only a long swell remained. Clear skies, the first for what seemed like weeks, helped to make the evening hours some of the most pleasant of the Southern Ocean so far. The Southern Cross, high in the sky as the sun set, reminded me of my remote southerly position. The wind died out completely just before darkness set in and at last I was able to take the yankee down and reinforce the leech line pocket which by now had almost disintegrated from heavy flogging. Using sticky Dacron and sewing the edges down with inch-long stiches I had the sail reset in fifteen minutes and at that moment along came a gentle breeze which had *Group 4* sailing smoothly after what had proved to be a grand prix-style pit stop. During the night we got into an amazing groove, sailing at over 8 knots in just 11 knots of breeze, a remarkable speed for a heavy yacht in light airs. A bright straight trail of bioluminescence marked our track through the water. It was a quiet night and a chance to sleep well and make miles at the same time.

As the sun rose I set the spinnaker and enjoyed a rare period of downwind sailing with a north-east breeze for most of the day. The times of sunrise and sunset were changing quickly now, becoming later and later each day as we began to make real westwards progress. Soon the time would advance so far that I would lose a day crossing the date line at 180° West. During the day the wind changed back to the more normal westerlies, quickly rising to 25 knots. Reefs and tacks kept me busy. I re-stowed the heavy gear and sails to improve the trim of the yacht and to help reduce the slamming and improve the performance. Moving this gear was never easy. Even the lightest spinnaker was a pig to move around below decks and involved rolling, pushing and kicking the sail into position which always left me exhausted. Once, in the middle of moving a spinnaker, I lay down on it and fell fast asleep halfway down the companionway. I tried to keep the weight aft and would use the diesel and water tanks in a sequence to bring the trim to what I considered to be the optimum for the yacht – any little thing to get me home faster.

The single sideband radio was now full of Indonesian banter. I could hear Sydney Radio very clearly but could not seem to cut through the other voices using the same frequencies. All these calls seemed to have the same characteristic tones, an agitated man shouting down the airwaves to a disinterested drawling female. It seemed unbelievable that the same people could be using the radio for so many hours of the day but whenever I dialled Sydney's frequencies there they would be, blocking any hope of contacting the outside world.

The head winds and currents continued but on 17th January, fifty-eight days out from Southampton, I received a telex from HQ. I had lost track of performance comparisons and Group 4's Control kindly supplied the information that I had finally drawn level with Chay, having caught him up by thirty-six days since Southampton. Chay's average speed was 4.1 knots to this point and mine had been 6.6 knots. This was pleasing but even more surprising was the news I was also three days ahead of *Group 4's* elapsed time on the fully crewed race. With better weather and no detour to Rio I knew the comparison was slightly unfair. But I also knew my averages were dropping day by day now, so this was a marvellous boost. I celebrated our success so far with a large Drambuie, then another. It was set to be a good day. I found a bumper bag full of unopened presents in the locker normally reserved for cornflakes. So I enjoyed a second somewhat belated Christmas and sent a thank you telex to those people who must have wondered why I had been so rude as not to thank them for the books, games, puzzles and barrel of brandy before now.

The next day, after repeated attempts, I finally got a clear link with Sydney Radio and was able to call Ceri. It was good to be able to have a long and cheering chat, and a pleasant change to exercise my voice in conversation rather than talking to myself.

The head winds built to a full gale from the north-west as the barometer fell and *Group 4* began to pound to windward again, heading south-west. I was busy repairing one of the Frederiksen cars on the mainsail. The 12 mm stainless steel bar which connected the car to the batten pocket had bent from the compression loads. Waves crashed on board as I struggled to change the fitting, standing on the winches on the side of the mast. The seas grew quickly and the skies looked especially leaden as I returned to the relative safety of the cockpit. The seas were frightening now and the barometer had not stopped its rapid fall. Moments later a huge backless wave left *Group 4* in mid-air. I dropped to my haunches, hands over my head and cowered behind the wheel as the sickening crash of the hull hitting the trough reverberated through hull and rig.

Moments later the boat went wildly off course as the port pilot packed up. A huge sea towered 300 yards off the starboard bow, the top tumbling as it met with a cross-sea and kept building. Before I could do anything with the helm, which was disconnected, it was on us. *Group 4* didn't have a chance to rise up over it as she normally did and, realising the danger I was in, I just slumped to the floor again. When the crash came I peered forward through the spokes of the wheel wide-eyed, and watched the mast invert alarmingly just above the aft lowers before everything was engulfed in solid blue freezing water. The cockpit was full and I hardly dared to look around. I had never seen the mast in such danger of breakage, despite two broken forestays the previous year.

On deck things stayed together well and the mast looked straight, but almost immediately the wind shot up to 45, then 50 knots and, grabbing the helm, I steered for several hours, feathering *Group 4* up to the wind in the gusts. Eventually, I was able to lash the wheel and the boat settled into steering herself through an amazing seascape. Below was a nightmare. Cupboards had burst open again, stowage boxes were scattered in the companionway. A pan of left-over chicken stew had found its way on to every surface in the galley area. It smelt revolting and the floor was an ice rink of greasy water and gravy. The cooker hob had jumped out its mount and was in pieces, the low battery alarm was sounding, together with the 'drive-cut' klaxon for the defunct pilot. Even the normally reliable Inmarsat had lost the West Atlantic signal and was beeping for attention. Finally the generator gave up and when I tried to start the main engine to put some charge in the batteries, the engine start batteries were dead.

I switched over the battery banks and was greatly relieved when the comforting sound of the main engine sprang to life. The generator cooling water pump had failed and the thermal cut-out had shut the diesel motor off to prevent further damage. I set to work changing the pump impeller for a spare and within an hour had the motor running again. Seconds later one of the supposedly unbreakable pump belts broke with the increased load of the new impeller and I fiddled around with the tiny watch-like components to fit a new belt before the unit was fully functional again. The pilot motor seemed to have terminally failed. A few days before I had changed the motor brushes and now moisture had gummed up the windings with the carbon dust left by the old worn brushes. The secondary pilot still worked but with conditions so bad I decided to not risk damaging that one. The boat seemed to steer herself fine whilst hard on the wind.

For a time the wind settled back to a steady 35 knots and, though the seas remained vicious, I began to tidy the mess below. A few hours later, in the middle of the night, the wind eased back to 18 knots, the barometer began rising again, and stars were clearly visible through breaks in the cloud. I went on deck to shake the reef and when easing the pennant out, I watched in horror as the three-quarter-inch fibreglass batten just above the third reef shattered and split four inches from the mast. During the worst of the wind I had wound in too much halyard tension to flatten the sail. Now easing the pennant had put all the halyard tension into batten compression, shattering the inboard end.

I dropped the sail and went below to get the tools and spares. In that few moments the wind was back up to gale force. The next three hours, till early light, were spent doing a job which is tricky enough on the dock, never mind alone and bucking along in 35 knots of wind in big seas and in pitch darkness. I tried to replace the bent connecting rod to the batten car but there were no spares, so I eventually had to butcher one of the spare cantilever car fittings for a spare component. It had been a bad few days but the problems only stiffened my resolve. I certainly had not been bored and the up side was the boat had survived a very bad storm without any serious difficulties. The autopilot failure was disconcerting at the time, but after a clean up with spirit the motor worked as well as ever.

I always felt a rising panic when something went wrong with the pilot system, far more so than with any other piece of kit on the boat. In 1988 I sailed one third of the distance across the Atlantic in the Single-handed Transatlantic Race with a broken autopilot. Handling a 30-foot trimaran without self-steering (or any electronics) was exhausting and I have few clear recollections of the last weeks of sailing. I was forced to stop at St John's in Newfoundland to repair a cracked beam to a float joint and arriving after such a prolonged period of wakefulness, in thick fog and uncertain of my exact position, was an experience I did not care to repeat – especially on this scale.

Handling *Group 4* without the benefit of good self-steering did not bear thinking about. Somehow Chay had managed when his self-steering failed on *British Steel*. In his book he seemed totally unfussed by the failure. *Group 4* would sail well without self-steering when she was going to windward but was hopeless if the wind drew further aft or dropped below 20 knots. My respect for Chay's achievement, especially without the self-steering, grew day by day.

By now I was starting to feel ground down by the weather. Progress seemed desperately slow and I was exhausted by the past days' worries and problems. I felt low on energy and was not eating well. An ear infection added to the growing list of physical irritations. My split tooth, which had been quiet up until now, began to ache. It wasn't a nice thought, spending the remaining months at sea with tooth and ear ache. My uncle's tooth-repair kit had repeatedly failed to cover the exposed sensitive break. In desperation I mixed some quick-setting epoxy glue and wiped it into the crack. The thought of waking with my jaw glued together made sleep difficult – but I was tired – and with a cotton-wool wad holding ear drops in my ear and a film container in my mouth to stop me clenching my teeth I slept uneasily. I must have looked a curious sight, but at least there was no one but Griselda to comment on the fact. The weather eased and when I woke I felt better. The glue had hardened and my ear had stopped aching. The tooth never caused another problem and after repeated applications of drops the ear drained and began to feel better.

I was now approaching the position on the planet that is noted in the *Guinness Book of Records* as the most remote place in all the world's oceans – 48°30′ South 125°30′ West is nearly 1,700 miles from the nearest land, a desolate cape on Antarctica, and many thousands of miles from any real port. I was now using the charts on which we had plotted the positions of the various rival Challenge yachts the year before. We had done a lot of close reaching in this area during that race. By contrast my track had been a jagged series of tacks for the past thousand miles – the longest beat ever.

I was still in fairly regular contact with *Cardiff Discovery*, but now reception was getting very poor. In our final contact before they faded out completely, they were obviously experiencing light airs as they approached the equator – I would have gladly swopped frustrations. The gales continued and a grey depressing fog descended. Although there was no reported ice in the area, it was hard not to imagine the ghosts of huge icebergs as I stared into the blankness feet ahead of the bows. How much time would I have? Would I be able to take avoiding action? I stopped looking and adopted a fatalistic approach.

A loud bang and flogging sail cloth gave me a fright during the night of the 22nd. For a moment I believed the inner forestay had failed. In fact, the staysail sheet had parted, leaving the sail flogging with a noise like gunfire. After 'end for ending' the sheet and part furling the sail, I turned in again. Despite using the heaters, everything still became damp, cold and uncomfortable. Nothing seemed to dry out completely. Layers of damp thermals, then wet foulies, and the now essential leather gloves, that felt like wearing a very slimy fish skin, did not improve the desire to get out there and get on with the ever present deckwork or maintenance. Comfort was measured by the littlest things which ashore would be unnoticed, a dry item of clothing, warm feet or a hot drink.

My average daily mileages were down to a hundred nautical miles or less. It seemed an age since I had put in a really good day's run. The main had been reefed now for almost two weeks and the eternal crashing and banging of the hull and the shaking of the rigging and sails ground away at morale. In my diary I wrote, 'I don't seem to have developed grey hair yet, I think the grey ones have probably all fallen out.'

On the 24th a belt of high pressure swept across my track, the barometer rose and the sky broke up, showing a glimmering of sunshine and, with it, the wind eased and shifted unfavourably west. I shook out one reef, a little headsail, relaxing to enjoy my morning coffee and toast as low cloud swept fast overhead. Two hours later the wind built and the barometer started a rapid fall again. Thirty minutes later I was back on deck taking in sail and tacking south-west again.

It was hard to believe the next breakage on deck, the supposedly super-strong staysail car on the port side sheared along its full length and pulled clean off the track – the steel deck around the track had lifted slightly, a measure of the strain everything was under, pounding through these seas. The car on the starboard side had also cracked and I replaced both with the spare cast bronze genoa cars. The loads placed on these sails and their gear is huge. I often ran the staysail sheets to the most powerful winches on the boat, the Lewmar 66s which are the biggest ones in the Lewmar range, as I simply could not wind the sail in properly in the stronger conditions using the normal staysail winches.

At this stage of the Challenge Race the crews were working flat out. Then our progress across the Southern Ocean was remarkable, surprising the critics and everyone, even us. Now I could still see my averages falling back. I had wrongly thought that my performance upwind would be nearly as good as that on the Challenge Race because the furling gear seemed to give infinite options, whereas downwind I thought I would be hindered by the heavy spinnaker gear. In reality it was proving to be precisely the opposite. The 24-knot limit on carrying headsails and the inefficiency of part furled sails slowed the boat. Whereas downwind my confidence with the spinnakers had increased to the point that performance was only limited to how hard I was willing to push the boat.

Finally, on 25th January as *Group 4* pressed north-west, a break in the weather gave some relief and the morning brought a beautiful bright day with clear skies and warm sunshine, the wind eased right down and, although we still punched through a head sea, it made a wonderful change. I ate breakfast basking in the warm sun in the cockpit with full sail set. A low, smoke-like mist rolled in from the north-west and, while it remained clear overhead, the visibility and temperature at sea level dropped dramatically. The wind dropped further and after all my whining about getting a break or some calm weather, a few hours was the most I could stand. I tacked south yet again, away from the high pressure and in search of a little more wind. Within an hour the wind was backing and building again, and the seas began to allow better progress.

This break was set to last and *Group 4* headed straight down the track. The gusty easterly wind shifted often and, with the spinnaker set, I spent hours attending the sail to prevent it either blowing or wrapping on the forestay. I loved the progress and, realising it was unlikely to last, I worked hard to get the best out of it. The mist turned to thick fog again and huge swells rolled in from the west as we made bumpy progress towards New Zealand, the spinnaker collapsing and refilling with a crack as the sail suffered from the strange wind against swell motion.

On day 67 my hand had become infected again. This, and the appearance of nasty boils on my arm, back and neck, prompted me to start a course of antibiotics and vitamins. To have become ill at this stage would have been terrible. I had learned the hard way that self-preservation was as important as preserving the boat's equipment. The trouble was the food had become quite limited in variety by now. There seemed to be a lack of savoury snacks and to compensate I baked ever more bread, sometimes adding salt and olive oil for the more savoury taste I craved. It was so cold, even below, that the dough would not rise unless I placed it in with the generator when I was charging the batteries.

The favourable wind built further and the following day I changed the spinnaker for a poled out yankee and began to put in some serious mileage. The average since Cape Horn had seemed slow but with the mileage creeping back over 200 miles a day it improved quickly. Not only was I pulling out from Chay, but now I was bringing my overall averages closer to those we had achieved on the Challenge Race. I slept well during this downwind period. After three weeks of working around the boat at a constant angle of heel it was wonderful to be able to put something down on the table without holding one hand ready to stop it from flying across the cabin. I felt worn down but generally fit after what already seemed like an eternity of hard upwind sailing.

I spoke to Philip on the 27th. Getting through to Sydney had become much easier. I was definitely closing the distance now and felt a rising excitement at the prospect of passing the halfway point. Looking back on my diary entries, it's easy to see just how rapid my mood swings were at this time, often directly linked to the daily mileages and the state of the weather. Now I felt great, encouraged and confident, while the weather worked with me. New Zealand didn't look so far away.

A shocking crash shook through the boat to her keelbolts. In a flash I was wide awake with frightening thoughts of icebergs or finding the rig over the side. The boat jerked upright, then began to heel quickly to starboard. I realised what had happened. The wind had shifted around behind us and *Group 4*, following a compass heading, had gybed all standing in 35 knots of wind. The boom preventer parted just as I reached the deck. I ducked below again as all hell let loose, the boom sweeping across collapsed several stanchions with the trailing preventer. To be hit by a boom or trailing rope the size of those on *Group 4* would not so much leave you unconscious as remove your head. The gybe could have left all sorts of damage – a broken boom or gooseneck, torn mainsail, smashed battens, even a broken mast. But *Group 4*'s considerable reserves of strength again prevented anything more than superficial damage. I sorted the mess of tangled trailing warps and went below for a coffee and some much needed breakfast energy. The wind continued to rise and later in the morning I climbed to the cockpit just to look at conditions and have a cigarette. The cockpit is generally a safe place in almost all conditions and in my thermals I was not wearing a harness. *Group 4* began to surf on a large wave, the frequency of the wave fitted the boat perfectly and we accelerated sharply.

Then I could hear the pilot struggling to get the helm round to prevent a broach. It didn't make it, and the boat began vibrating as the speed rose and she began a nasty death roll to port. Blue, solid water was beginning to pile over the bows and along the side deck. There was no time to think and, in a kamikaze bid to not be around when she went all the way, I hurled myself headlong through the main hatch. I couldn't help thinking, as I flew through the air, that I had done this little manoeuvre once before – seconds before *Gazelle*, a 30-foot trimaran I was racing in the Round Britain and Ireland Race, capsized in a severe gale off the Shetland Islands.

It's a good four-foot drop inside the main hatch, and I landed hard, but safe, on the cabin sole next to the chart table. The max. speed indicator was showing 17.8 knots as a blue water wave, having travelled over the bows past the mast and back to the cockpit, hit the hatch canopy so hard it slid shut with a bang, cracking the fibreglass edges. A few moments later, and more properly dressed with full foulies and harness, I put the deep reef in, a tricky operation as downwind the enormous wind pressure forced the sail back against the rig, making it very difficult to haul down, but I managed this by alternately winding in the reefing pennant and easing the halyard and the sail came down remarkably smoothly.

Feeling lucky if bruised, I went below again to nurse the freshly opened cuts on my hands. The new skin had just peeled back and they were back to square one, but another month of sore hands was probably a small price to pay, considering the alternative of being swept over the back of the boat.

Later I spoke to Charles on the radio to discuss the logistics of shifting the next rendezvous from New Zealand to Tasmania. It still seemed miles ahead, but it was great to be even thinking about it. Because there were too few alternatives for an easy rendezvous point off New Zealand's South Island, I had decided on Tasmania, which would also force me to sail a more northerly track across the Indian Ocean – no bad thing! So we agreed on this shift of the goal posts which had several other advantages as far as I was concerned. Tasmania had been the Challenge crew's favourite stopover and, in many respects, it felt like heading for home waters. It was also both the psychological and physical halfway mark. I was now about a thousand miles from passing through the shallow water between New Zealand and Auckland Island. A good week's sailing was still ahead.

With the prospect of meeting people soon, I couldn't help noticing in the mirror how dishevelled I looked. A thin ginger beard had grown and my hair was long and untidy. A shower, then a haircut saw me looking and feeling much better and I surprised myself by not doing a bad job with the scissors and thinking that if I had come out of a barber's looking like that I would probably only complain, not sue.

Antipodes Island and Bounty Island lay just ahead of my track, names that conjured up thoughts of tropical sun, sand and palm trees, but of course these islands, squarely in the roaring forties and the freezing cold waters of the Southern Ocean Current, are as far from the TV chocolate bar commercials as you can get. After so many miles of relaxed navigation with nothing to avoid, I now stepped up the frequency of log entries and plots. With the thousands of miles of open ocean between Cape Horn and New Zealand there had been little point in plotting a position every day. I had read of other solo sailors who ended up either hitting reefs or running up beaches after long ocean crossings. Now I could see just how easily it might happen.

Progress began to falter again on 31st January as the wind became squally and shifted back and forth as much as twenty degrees either side of the course line. In conditions like this it was nearly impossible to settle down to rest, read or cook, the wind-shift or off-course alarms continually sounded through the boat. I learnt to sleep in catnaps with the Raytheon hand-held controls for the autopilot tucked under my pillow. Like this I could silence the alarms and alter course, keeping an eye on the changes from the comfort of my sleeping bag. I had hardened to the deckwork since Cape Horn, but still found the repeated heavy winch grinding difficult, a job often shared by two or even three crew members. Though I paced myself through each sail change to prevent muscle strains or injuries, the bumps and scrapes of recent weeks, together with a couple of other minor ailments, conspired to make life very uncomfortable. Unbelievably, I had forgotten to bring any simple antiseptic cream. But I would wash my injuries regularly in liquid soap surgical scrub, and this helped to keep serious infection at bay.

As for the boat, minor problems or just straightforward wear and tear caused by the continual pounding appeared daily. I became very aware of the fact that even a simple fault in one of the essential systems could change the character of the voyage immediately. But overall the boat was confirming its reliability. I was the weak link, and I knew it, so it was down to me to take proper care of myself physically. Mentally and emotionally I was feeling in good nick and genuinely unaffected by the length of time at sea alone. Of course I wanted to finish and never a day went past without my dreaming of an end to the relentless battle against the weather. Now the prospect of reaching Tasmania and the halfway stage spurred me along. I missed my friends and company but it wasn't so much a feeling of loneliness as one of boredom that assailed me in the occasional quiet moments. To compensate for the lack of external stimulation I would spend hours tuning in to hear what was going on in the outside world. BBC World Service was normally audible for several hours a day and I became an avid follower of many of the programmes, no matter how bad the reception. I would also listen to music or to the language tapes I had been given for Christmas. I jumped out of my skin a couple of times when the *Teach Yourself Spanish* tape came on unexpectedly as it auto-reversed when I came down from the deck. And, the last resort of the single-handed, I talked to myself quite often, particularly during the deckwork, when a bit of self-encouraging chat helped to ensure I got things right when I was feeling tired. When conditions were really bad I would go along the side deck repeating a simple mantra, 'I must not fall over the side', again and again.

7

Tasman Rendezvous
(Day 73 – Day 84)

On 1st February, seventy-three days out, a bright moonlit night saw *Group 4* zigzagging through sparkling seas between latitude 47° South and 48° South, but the head winds had slowed progress and our average speed, which had risen during the last bout of favourable wind, was now slipping back again.

The view on deck was astonishing. Clouds on the horizon rose from just a few hundred to tens of thousands of feet like dozens of floating Mount Everests, their flanks lit by the crystal clear star-filled skies and, with the kite-shape of the Southern Cross in the south and Orion's Belt ahead to the west, the view was truly spectacular.

Beneath the clouds intense squalls left sharp images on the radar, more solid in appearance than any ship or land mass. They had me peering into the darkness under the clouds to make sure that nothing really was bearing down on us. Wind shifts of fifty degrees were not uncommon and the wind could rise as much as 20 knots in a few seconds, making us alternately heavily over-pressed or underpowered. Torrential rain and hail fell in sheets, hitting the deck so hard that the from below it sounded more like living under a corrugated tin roof. On deck, the sheer force of water falling out of the sky took one's breath away.

Although still over 600 miles from passing under New Zealand, I found myself already jockeying for the correct position to catch the best line to pass, more as one might fight for position on an inshore race. I enjoyed spending time looking for the favourable tack, or trying to work the weather systems as they hurtled past. This was more of a mind game to pass the time, as the favourable tack was normally obvious. I found it very difficult to sleep whenever the wind offered no favourable option and would sit endlessly in the nav. station waiting for a shift one way or the other. The weatherfaxes showed the major depressions filing across towards me but often these larger systems would be made up of a series of smaller systems. Despite the weatherfax technology and the computing powers of Metroute at Bracknell, I relied more heavily on the barometer and cloud observations for short-term forecasting.

I spoke to Dr Campbell Mackenzie on the radio. As crew member on *Rhône Poulenc* during the Challenge Race, he had become the fleet doctor and he had helped me put together a very comprehensive medical kit. Now he advised and reassured me about some of the minor medical problems which had become a worry. Our discussion got round to diet, and when confronted with it, I had to admit that some of the food which had seemed desirable when victualling the boat, now seemed virtually unpalatable and I had started to skip proper meals. Since Cape Horn I had been losing weight, not quickly, but steadily. I needed to step up my calorie intake and eat a more varied diet – not just my favourites. I longed for a good steak and fresh salad.

Finally, I crossed the international date line. The 2nd February 1994 did not occur on *Group 4*. I understood the theory of it, but the reality took some getting used to. From here onwards I would be counting down the degrees of east longitude and, in a way, I felt I was now on the downhill run towards home.

I passed twenty miles to the south of Bounty Island, a desolate lump of weathered rock, unpopulated and covered with guano. The whole island is swept clean during the winter months by enormous Southern Ocean waves that can crash from one side of the island to the other. Now I was approaching New Zealand several new species of bird were around the boat, one of them, the Elliot's petrel, continually tiptoeing across the waves in the odd purposeless way petrels do. I seldom saw these birds actually feeding. The big wandering albatrosses that had been with the boat on and off all the way from Cape Horn were still around us daily, dwarfing all other birds and seldom setting down to feed or rest. Albatrosses and petrels are truly oceanic birds and in the winds of the Southern Ocean they are totally in their element. They relish the bad weather and, no matter how fierce the wind, they looked ever more graceful as they glided effortlessly, back and forth, across *Group 4*'s wake. The Pacific Southern Ocean had been pretty well devoid of sea life, a few dolphins after Cape Horn, but otherwise nothing. It should be one of the cleanest oceans on the planet and I hoped it was just the fact of the millions of square miles it covered that made sightings less frequent.

The following night both the autopilots failed one after the other. I was getting into my sleeping bag when the boat slewed off course with the sails flogging wildly and the boom crashing back and forth. I ran on deck dressed only in my underwear and, after getting the boat sailing again, I lashed the helm, but not before I had received a thorough drenching in freezing Southern Ocean. I went below and began the search for the cause of the problem, first crawling into the tiny electrical locker under the nav. station with a circuit tester. It was a pitch black night with around 25 knots of winds from the west, a heavy swell and violent squalls. Back on deck, I rigged some lighting over the hydraulic self-steering unit, re-trimming the wheel from time to time. The port pilot relief valve had failed again and I replaced that with a spare. Looking at the starboard pilot, the fault appeared to be the motor brushes again, and following Autohelm's advice, I took the motor to bits and cleaned the brush mountings. Steve at Autohelm had made it sound simple, but working under Southern Ocean conditions, I was soon covered in the fine black carbon powder and quite unable to get the wretched thing back together. It was more like a Krypton Factor puzzle. The strong magnets in the commutator foiled every attempt to line up the securing screws. After an hour of trying I gave up for the night. By now there were tools and bits everywhere, the carbon dust powder had spread itself around the boat and it began to rain and blow even harder. I began to feel even more despondent as I started to pack away, when the generator ran out of fuel, the fuel transfer pump broke and the Inmarsat dumped all the day's files and the start of a daily diary for no apparent reason.

I sorted it all out, bit by bit, fitting a complete spare pilot motor

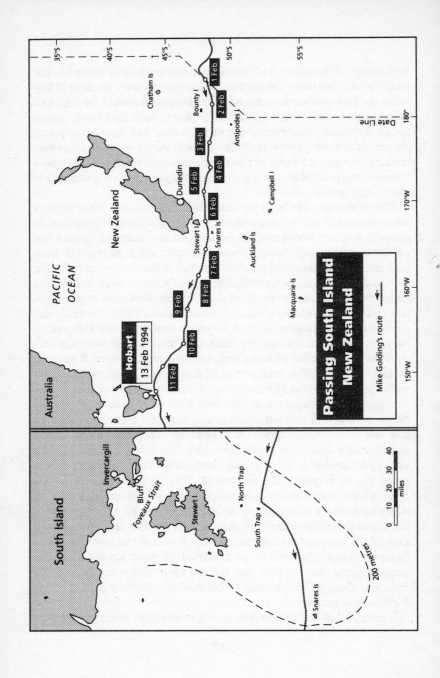

Passing South Island
New Zealand

Mike Golding's route ------

Hobart
13 Feb 1994

35°S
40°S
45°S
50°S
55°S

Chatham Is
Bounty I
Antipodes
Dunedin
Campbell I
Stewart I
Snares Is
Auckland Is
Macquarie Is

1 Feb
2 Feb
3 Feb
4 Feb
5 Feb
6 Feb
7 Feb
8 Feb
9 Feb
10 Feb
11 Feb

New Zealand
Australia

PACIFIC OCEAN

Date Line
180°
170°W
160°W
150°W

South Island

Invercargill
Bluff
Foveaux Strait
Stewart I
North Trap
South Trap
Snares Is

200 metres

0   10   20   30   40
miles

rather than finish the puzzle – I would save that for a rainy day. I now only had one spare pilot valve left, a component which had already failed twice. I refused to heave to to sort these problems. As long as I could keep moving down the track I did. Stopping for any reason seemed unthinkable, it would be the start of a decline towards giving up, so I had to keep moving. By the time I had finished packing away and wiped away the worst of the brush powder, the sun was just rising. I reduced sail to ensure less likelihood of a disturbance and crashed out in the saloon.

The wind was not kind, the regular squalls from the west kept progress to a minimum. Whichever way I turned, the wind seemed to know and follow me round, making the new course unfavourable. The remaining 300 miles to New Zealand were proving slow and testing. The main evidence of progress was that radio reception was improving day by day, and I was able to link up through Sydney Radio for media interviews on most days. Perhaps the most frequently asked questions implied that, as I was now over a month ahead of Chay, the remainder of the passage was going to be a foregone conclusion. I hated this as, with the various problems growing, I believed the next half of the passage was to be the most likely time to fail, and it was down to me to work harder than ever to keep everything going and make the maximum daily mileages.

I started to put on the navigation lights at night again now. In mid-ocean it had been a waste of power and the main reason for using the light had been to back-light the Windex (which had since fallen off). The likelihood of a ship's path crossing mine along a route so far south and off all regular shipping lanes had been very remote. Nights were exceptionally black now, the moon rose just before dawn each day. To make matters worse the deck light bulb blew, so deckwork had to be done with a torch. Replacing the sealed beam unit, thirty feet off the deck with the yacht bouncing along, was just too risky. Getting myself up the mast with the four-part purchase was proving harder than I had expected. I found it almost impossible to go higher than the second spreaders, part fear and part the state of my hands preventing me. My hands bled and swelled badly after any attempt.

On day 77 a high pressure system slid south-east over us, the wind dropped out and in the afternoon bright warm sunshine on a smooth sea gave me a chance to strip some of the thermal layers off, wash clothes and watch the hundreds of birds that had gathered around the boat. I hauled the light spinnaker out of its Southern Ocean stowage in the depths of the three-berth cabin, and *Group 4* drifted along at 3 knots with it scarcely filling. In the distance, I could just see the shadow of Stewart Island south of Invercargill. A group of rocks ahead called North and South Trap forced me to sail very deep downwind at an inefficient wind angle, as I struggled to avoid the need for a series of time-consuming gybes between them.

The quieter weather allowed me to resume progress with the ever growing list of maintenance and repairs and today my list included – strip the day tank pump, locate generator starting problem and clean the earth strap connection, fit a new sealed beam unit in the deck light, clean the heads, pump the sump tank, fit new pilot motors, repair one of the old motors, change watermaker filters (clogged with plankton), change gas bottles, refit three broken off cupboard doors and wash my thermals.

Now both pilots were working well again, I treated all the components with a care more suited to watch repair and made plastic cowlings to give the last relief valves more weather protection. The motors had been suffering from the continual slamming loads that kicked back through the steering system. The commutators had smashed through the washers that were supposed to prevent them from sliding back and forth inside the housing. I replaced the washers with stronger filed down penny washers which gave no further problems. The relief valve failures were more worrying. I had the port pilot valve working again, but these valves had few components and could not be repaired. As far as I was concerned when the last valve blew, there would be no more autopilot – it was a thought I did not dwell on. I found one of the spare gas bottles was empty, which meant it had either been loaded empty or its contents had leaked away. I began to take more care about how I used gas. I boiled a kettle twice a day, filling a thermos flask to save constantly using the stove.

And so on day 79 I passed out of the Pacific Southern Ocean and into the Tasman Sea with Storm Bay and the Tasmania rendezvous 850 miles ahead. The light airs dispersed during the night, shifting from east to north, and increasing in strength. By morning the reefs started to go back in, as the wind continued to back towards west and rise towards gale force. This wind shift allowed me to clear South Trap rock easily, passing five miles to the south, then, as it continued to back, Snares Islands became the next obstruction. I passed very close to the north of the group in the late afternoon. This was my first clear sight of land since Cape Horn, and the sheer-cliffed, multi-peaked islands looked equally forbidding, even in bright sunshine.

As the islands drew astern the seas suddenly became very steep-sided and short, making the convergence boundary between the Pacific Ocean and the Tasman Sea. Within a few miles, as I got back into deeper water, the sea settled into a more regular pattern, but distinctly different from that of the Pacific Southern Ocean. Strangely, the birds that had surrounded the boat for the past few days had disappeared, perhaps preferring to stay in the lee of New Zealand's South Island. The Tasman Sea had a totally different feel to it. It was a welcome change after the monotonous conditions of the Southern Ocean. I would have to head south again after the Tasmania rendezvous but for now it was a wonderful feeling to know that I had proved, to myself at least, that it was possible to sail a Challenge yacht in the Southern Ocean alone.

The wind built to a near gale on the night of day 80, and I worked to put the deep reef in the mainsail. The sea and swell were so different that I needed to be extra careful. I had become accustomed to a system of working around the mast, knowing instinctively where and when to clip on, or how to prevent tangles in the reefing pennants, and the changed motion now caught me unawares. It was not worse, just different, coming from both the north and west, making the seas sharper and shorter. Heavy fog had descended by the morning and the wind eased away again. Perhaps because he followed a more northerly route, Chay seemed to suffer repeated calms in the Southern Ocean. Each time the wind dropped I would race around trying to get the best out of the boat with the last of the breeze. I had expected to park up for days but it just had not happened yet.

I packed the Pacific charts away and began to look through those for the Indian Ocean. I still had not decided on a route but knew I did not wish to sail so far south in the Indian Ocean. I had had a rough passage across the Pacific and felt no great desire to risk damage by heading straight towards the extreme conditions found in the Southern Indian Ocean. I knew that after Tasmania things could become markedly worse. The routing chart indicated that a more northerly track than that taken on the Challenge Race might give better wind angles, allowing me to sail closer to the course line for more of the time. Sailing any further north risked lengthy calms and I watched the weatherfax daily to try and see a pattern of movement in the Indian Ocean high pressure system. Weather observations for some of the wind roses on the statistical routing chart were few and far between, making historical information unreliable.

The only other option was to head towards the south-west corner of Australia and try to sail over the top of the Indian Ocean high, crossing at roughly 32° South. This was an attractive option, as it would mean long periods of trade wind sailing and fair weather. However, the mileage, even on the shortest possible route over the high pressure, was over a thousand miles longer than a more southerly crossing. To make this worthwhile, I would need to be able to sail consistently fifteen to twenty per cent faster. Fine if the boat could avoid calms. But the only certainty was the consistent winds of the roaring forties and this was the route I believed I needed to take. We had compiled a file full of statistical and historical weather routing information which had been researched for the Challenge Race. With this and the practical experience gained during that race, it was interesting to try slightly different routes or methods of getting the best out of each weather system. There are really very few hard and fast rules and I only ever viewed this as an overall strategy. Day to day decisions based on actual observation always gave more significant results.

The Indian Ocean produced the worst weather during the Challenge Race and the chapter describing this part of Chay's voyage was called 'The Worst Ocean'. On *Group 4* last time we had recorded twenty-eight days of gale-force winds out of the thirty-three days it took from Hobart to Cape Town. I felt more confidence in the boat than ever, but was becoming increasingly apprehensive at the prospect of the Southern Indian Ocean. So far the equipment failures and injuries had been little more than an inconvenience but I knew that just one serious failure or mistake could still put an end to my ambitions. Messages from home indicated that everyone was beginning to feel the record was a foregone conclusion. I was far less certain.

The weather changed even more rapidly than usual in the Tasman. The proximity to land stirred up smaller but more powerful weather systems that gave alternate calms, beats and fast-reaching conditions. Approaching Tasmania I had to struggle to keep up but all the same enjoyed the break from the monotony of the Pacific Ocean. With conditions so changeable, it was easy to see how so many seafaring superstitions arose as protection against the fickle changes of weather. When I studied at Lowestoft Nautical College, I worked for a short time on the North Sea trawlers. Not whistling on board is a reasonably well-known superstition, but on the trawlers some of the rougher characters would threaten actual bodily harm to anyone caught whistling because whistling up the wind would spoil the catch. I still hate people whistling aboard a yacht – one can't be too careful. This never seemed a totally unreasonable superstition. One that I never did understand, though, was the ban on mentioning pigs. An accidental slip of the P-I-G word could make those trawlermen turn very nasty. I became pretty careful what I said during meals.

The 9th February was a grey threatening sort of a day. Within an hour of putting the spinnaker up the wind slowly increased and we began to fly across an unusually smooth Tasman Sea. The easy ride allowed further work on the pilots' relief valves. They were sticking again and I took the opportunity to strip the two working valves down and clean the insides of the valve units. There was minimal corrosion inside the electrical coils and little sign of what had caused the failures. I received advice from Steve Moore of Autohelm but we were both at a loss to explain why the valves, which were supposed to be continuously rated, should be failing so quickly. The test bed valves back in the factory seemed to be working fine. With the exception of these hydraulic valves, I felt total confidence in the pilot system. After all, it had survived halfway around the world and performed superbly in all conditions. Ironically the valves were heavy duty ones, not the standard Autohelm component. Steve had changed to these after I had expressed concern over their wanting to use newer untested components.

On 10th February an impressive lightning storm kept me awake for most of night, while *Group 4* beat to windward in steep seas, shrouded in fog. As each flash of lightning lit the fog, a hundred-yard circle of spiky seas was illuminated around the yacht and sheets of mist scudded across the surface. Moments later, plunged back into darkness, an unbelievable crash of thunder shook the air.

Meanwhile in Hobart Rear Commodore Don Colbourn of the Royal Yacht Club of Tasmania was co-ordinating planning, and I was in daily radio communications with Jeff Boyes of the Yacht Club and Tas Coast Radio who kept me up to date with the arrangements for the BBC support boat and aircraft which would film *Group 4*'s passage. Shortly, too, I would be crossing paths with a host of other yachts on round-the-world events – all going the right way around. Jeff updated me on the Whitbread Race and the amazing progress of the new Open 60s versus the Maxis. Even more astonishing was that made by the big multihulls competing for the Jules Verne Trophy for rounding the world in less than eighty days. Robin Knox-Johnston and Peter Blake were co-skippering *Enza*, a 92-foot catamaran which had left the Channel on 16th January and was already deep in the Southern Ocean at longitude 60° East having maintained an incredible average speed of over 15 knots. We exchanged telexes and planned a radio schedule as we converged from opposite directions at a closing speed of over 20 knots. Their progress was a stark reminder of the relatively slow progress I was making, sailing uphill and alone.

I was changing the sail plan every few hours, and had been doing so since New Zealand. Heading north-west gave the prospect of better weather and, as I moved nearer Tasmania, bright spells became more frequent, making a pleasant change from the usual bleakness of southern seas. Seals appeared from time to time. Generally they seemed to be snoozing, flippers pointing skywards, soaking up the sun, often lying amongst islands of floating kelp, another sign of my proximity to land.

As the sun set on day 82 *Group 4* drifted towards the familiar shape of Tasman Head. The light spinnaker scarcely filled and a smooth sea with big rolling swells from the west slowed progress to a crawl. The BBC film crew's chartered aircraft approached from the north, flying low overhead, circling many times and filming the boat with the spectacular backdrop of the Organ Pipes, a prominent Basalt outcrop and a famous feature of the Tasmanian coastline. As the light faded Tony Rayner the BBC producer contacted me through Tas Coast Radio to make arrangements for another rendezvous further down the coast at Adventure Bay early next morning.

A frustrating night followed as a fair wind filled in but I needed to slow down to prevent myself from overshooting the rendezvous. Being so close to land meant sleep was sporadic at best. Tiredness and the intrusion into my day by day routine made me irritable to the point of anger. On the one hand I knew that Tony and the film crews had travelled halfway around the world record this moment; on the other it was the first time the sailing and PR requirements had clashed. I had originally looked forward to the rendezvous as a healthy break to the monotony. But now the need to achieve the best day's run possible on every day had become a total obsession, outweighing sociable diversions. I used the night hours to repair two damaged spinnakers which blocked the companionway and I cursed every wasted hour.

Sunrise found *Group 4* charging into Adventure Bay at over 10 knots. I was keen to get the filming done and be on my way again. The motorlaunch *Loon Gara* approached and together we headed into the deep cut in the rugged coastline to the south of Bruny Island, where the fresh wind vanished to nothing in seconds. The land provided the shelter needed to drop the film canisters and do the interviews. For an hour we were able to talk easily as the yacht drifted slowly back towards the open ocean. The frustrations of the previous night were forgotten and I enjoyed the meeting. Having been alone for nearly three months, it was just good to talk, face to face with people, and I only slipped into radiospeak a couple of times by saying 'over' at the end of a sentence.

Des Cooper, one of Hobart's leading surgeons, had come out specifically to advise me on some of the medical problems I was still experiencing. I had been feeling increasingly run down in the Southern Ocean and the outward effects, the slow healing and infected hand wounds, as well as the boils that had developed on my neck and back, were becoming more than a simple irritation. I had experienced similar problems on the Challenge Race and during the Hobart stopover Des had prescribed a course of antibiotics. The antibiotics I carried this time had proved ineffective but, of course, I could not accept the medicine that Des had brought with him. He looked surprised, but even this small item would have compromised the strict rules regarding outside assistance. 'Without assistance' means nothing can be taken on board – not even a pill. So instead he advised me on diet and ways to improve the natural healing properties of the body.

Eventually I became worried about getting out of the bay. With no wind *Group 4* had little steerage and the current began setting me on shore. Our remaining conversation continued as I coaxed the boat south, out of the island's wind shadow, under the newly repaired light spinnaker. Finally, we said our goodbyes. The *Loon Gara* headed back towards the friendly shores of Tasmania and I watched as they disappeared behind Bruny Island. Then, changing the spinnaker for headsails, I turned *Group 4* further south in an attempt to find the wind again.

The Tasman coast drifted lazily past, the weather was beautiful and, stripped to my shorts, I lapped up the sun whilst it lasted, though it was frustrating not to be able to get clear of the land quickly. An enormous high pressure system had built over Tasmania and Southern Australia and it was clearly going to be a couple of days before we really started to make progress again.

Several Tasmanian and Australian radio stations contacted the yacht for interviews, mostly through Jeff at Tas Coast Radio. I received loads of messages of support on the Inmarsat and was able to make good link calls with friends and family, something to take full advantage of after coming out of one long period of solitude and infrequent communication and now heading straight into another.

I planned to sail a composite route through the Indian Ocean passing to the south of Amsterdam Island. This would be a more northerly track than that sailed on the Challenge Race but, if the routing charts were correct, I could expect more favourable wind angles. The trick would be to stay away from the calms of the Indian Ocean high pressure zone which dominates the weather in the mid latitudes.

I gybed the spinnaker and headed south in search of more wind as the forecast and weatherfaxes showed a new system rushing in. As the barometer fell, a bank of cloud slowly slid across from the west and a long swell built but still no wind came. The shadow of Tasmania was still visible to the north-east as evening approached and the powerful navigation light on Maatsuyker Island swept across the horizon. Huge bursts of bioluminescence erupted around the yacht as we moved slowly away from the land lights towards South Africa, 6,800 miles away.

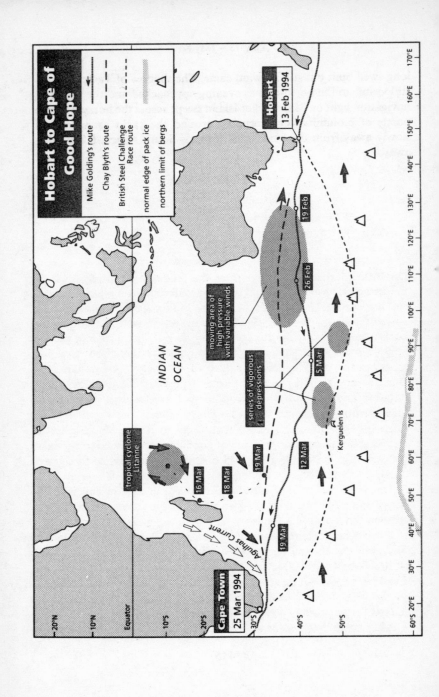

Hobart to Cape of Good Hope

- Mike Golding's route
- Chay Blyth's route
- British Steel Challenge Race route
- normal edge of pack ice
- northern limit of bergs

Hobart 13 Feb 1994

Cape Town 25 Mar 1994

INDIAN OCEAN

Equator

tropical cyclone Litanne

Aguilhas Current

moving area of high pressure with variable winds

series of vigorous depressions

Kerguelen Is

16 Mar
18 Mar
19 Mar
12 Mar
19 Mar
5 Mar
26 Feb
19 Feb

8

Gone West
(Day 85 – Day 99)

On 14th February, two days after the rendezvous, the forecast for moderate north-easterlies still had not materialised. I changed charts for the eastern part of the Southern Indian Ocean but Tasmania stayed frustratingly close, the daily positions moved just millimetres across the chart. At first light I gybed back to the west and put the light spinnaker up again. To keep occupied I immersed myself in maintenance, reading and listening to the radio. Australian news sounded much the same as the rest of the world's, unemployment, inflation and politicians up to no good. I gave several interviews to local stations and was startled to hear myself on a pre-recorded interview on ABC. Finally, I got through to Robin Knox-Johnston on *Enza*, but reception was still not good and we planned to try again the next day. They were in the flow of strong westerlies and flying, well ahead of schedule.

The wind picked up from the north-east on day 86 and with the heavy spinnaker set *Group 4* also flew, in our case south-west. The temperatures dropped suddenly and, with the wind swinging quickly to north-west, torrential rain cut visibility to a few hundred yards. The Southern Ocean was beginning to make itself felt again. The wind shifted back and forth, setting the windvane alarms ringing every time I laid my head down to rest and the boat would slew round erratically as the pilot tried to respond to sluggish compass readings, as we moved further south, nearer the magnetic South Pole.

After my daily schedule with Jeff at Tas Coast Radio, I managed to raise *Enza* clearly. They sounded in tremendous spirits and had reached 43° 15′ South 115° 57′ East, maintaining their 15-knot plus average. When I explained that I planned to bring the record for a solo east/west circumnavigation down to around 180 days, Robin's response was, 'Why restrict yourself to 180?' which was a fair comment and worth remembering!

Later I had to laugh when I opened former *Group 4* crew member Jim Barrett's parcel mysteriously marked 'Not to be opened until the day after Valentine's day'. I had imagined a sister for Griselda but it turned out to be a stress-relieving 'beat the wife' tear-apart doll with Velcro-attached arms, legs and head. I felt little stress on day 86, but the next day things changed for the worse dramatically.

First the starboard pilot failed, the relief valve blew as I had been dreading it might. I had been communicating with Steve at Autohelm about the possibility of extending the life of the valves by rewiring them to open with twelve volts rather than the normal twenty-four. He was also investigating ideas to get the pilots working without the valves, but I still had not received an answer. I sent a telex urging him to give me some suggestions, now!

Far more seriously, the generator had stopped giving any charge to the batteries. I carried out all the obvious test and checks with my electrical meter but the red charging indicator light refused to turn green as it should have. The little diesel motor still ran well, it was only the electrical side of the unit that seemed faulty and I believed that in time I would be able to repair it – after all it was only a few months old and I had a fairly comprehensive spares kit. I telexed Group 4 HQ seeking guidance from the supplier. In the short term I could charge the batteries with the main engine but with at least three months' sailing ahead, I did not believe the fuel would last. The main engine was a 120 hp Mermaid Ford diesel, a bus engine, it used six litres an hour, compared to the generator's two, a big difference in fuel consumption! I made plans for what could be done to reduce fuel consumption and started by switching off all non-essential electrics.

A gale had built from the south-west and the seas became so bad that I was unable to work on either the pilot or the generator during the night hours. I cooked a chicken stew instead and slept in the saloon, listening to the motor of the port pilot, waiting for that to fail

118

too. As daylight returned I couldn't stand the waiting any longer. I had to find out if the pilot and generator could be fixed. Covering the area behind the steering wheel with sail bags to protect both me and the pilots from spray, I set to work stripping the starboard pilot down. I felt so totally reliant on the pilots that I treated the components like the Holy Grail. Very carefully, bit by bit, I reassembled each unit. By midday I had them both working, one with the last spare valve, and the other with the original valve which I managed to get moving again by pressing its body back into shape in a vice. There were no more spares and these would need to go the whole distance. The most frustrating thing was the fact that in all other respects the pilots were working well – only these valves were causing real problems.

After a coffee and a Mars Bar, I tacked south and lashed the helm, conserving both the power and the pilot system. Then I started work on the generator. This was a far more involved job, I needed to remove the whole generator and motor assembly from its sound-proofed pod, turn it on its end, and remove the end plate to reveal the windings. All this in the confines of the wet locker and with the boat bucking and heaving in 25 knots of wind. After removing all the fuel lines, cooling water pipes, control cables and power feed wires, I loosened the mounting screws and heaved the small but very heavy motor round in the pod, fresh cuts and abrasions opening on my hands as I did so. Having removed the securing screws from the generator cover plate, I started to try to prise the cover off with a series of screwdrivers driven in around the sealed edge. It was really a job for specialist tools but after a frustrating hour the lid finally sprang off and my heart sank as the smell of burnt electrical insulation filled the cabin. Blackened water was visible inside the generator and the area of burnt wiring meant that I was probably wasting my time doing anything further. Still, I continued to clean and dry the coil and housing, treating it with the same reverence as the pilots. The gasket which prevented cooling water from entering the electrical coil had failed and to reassemble the unit I used a thick seal of Sikaflex sealant in place of a paper gasket. By dusk I was in a position to connect it up and give it another try. The supplier had given only a 50/50 chance of success. Feeling very despondent, I held rather less hope. I said a little prayer before hitting the button, and it started straight away. But the red panel light still indicated a fault and, as if to mark its final death knell, the new seal burst, sending a fountain of water across the wet locker.

I had just three tanks of fuel left and now needed to run the main engine several hours a day just to maintain minimum communications, navigation and autopilot systems. On the Challenge Race we ran the engine for up to six hours a day, but fuel was not a problem as we could refuel in each stopover.

As far as I was concerned now, the port pilot relief valve was almost certainly going to fail within the next week or so. The starboard pilot would last for some time as its valve was nearly new. I decided to run the old valve first. Every day it worked from here on would be a bonus day. I would need the working pilot for the Atlantic stage more than in the Southern Ocean. I had been experimenting with making the yacht steer herself by lashing the helm. She seemed to be quite happy sailing to windward in winds of more than 20 knots but would wander wildly off course when the wind strength dropped or moved further abeam. The prevailing conditions would for once be working to my advantage, preserving the pilot and power supply.

I began a series of checks on my fuel supply, a calculation complicated by the cross-filling between tanks through the breather pipes each time I tacked. It would have been so much simpler if the tanks had been fitted with external sight gauges. I was beginning to feel that things were going wrong far too quickly. I was heading into the 'worst ocean' short of fuel and with an autopilot system that was looking increasingly certain to fail. I felt depressed and wrote in my diary, 'I know this passage is supposed to be in Chay's wake, but this is ridiculous – strictly for the birds – a total mug's game – how the hell did I get here?' Then I added, on a more positive note, 'Still it ain't over till the fat lady sings.'

The following day I began thinking how to save fuel in earnest. Life aboard *Group 4* was about to become far more uncomfortable as I started to enforce a list of economy measures:

1 Inmarsat messages and polled positions reduced to one period per day.
2 All heating switched off.
3 All but three light bulbs removed below. Deck and nav. lights not used.

4 Radar and 50% of instrument systems disconnected.
5 One of the two GPS navigators shut down and the NMEA control cable changed over to enable the Inmarsat to give one daily position to HQ.
6 All radios turned off.
7 The lazy pilot ram disconnected.

Where I could disconnect something, I did. I wanted to remove all temptation to switch on a light or power up an instrument. From now on every minute I could reduce the power consumption would give me an extra minute before the fuel ran out. Meanwhile back in the UK the Challenge Business swung into action. Andrew Roberts and his team had started a series of clinical tests using the other identical Challenge yachts. Gara Hampton, the fleet engineer, was dispatched down to the yachts in Brixham to carry out direct tests of fuel consumption and to find the optimum throttle settings to get the most power for the least fuel. The two Lucas alternators had served us well during the Challenge Race and it was now going to be vital that they gave me their best performance.

The south-west wind was into its fourth day and, with the inefficiency of lashing the helm, my course had carried us too far north and dangerously close to the high pressure system. The wind began to drop to light on the 18th. At first I was quite relieved that the favoured tack was north going, I was starting to feel less than keen on the prospect of getting into any really bad weather. My resolve was badly shaken, the equipment failures were making me pessimistic and, for the first time, the prospect of not finishing seemed real. The Group 4 Global Challenge was one of many ambitions. I had been presented with all the right circumstances to have a go and I had grasped the opportunity. Until now I had just gone with it. But now *Group 4* and mother nature had conspired to present me with difficulties that posed the real question, 'Do I really want to finish?' I needed to decide and decide soon.

Chay had sailed across the whole Southern Ocean and back up the Atlantic without self-steering. I had set out to beat his record and now needed to live up to his example – I cursed him and his tenacity. Philip Sørensen and Group 4 had taken a considerable risk in backing the Global Challenge. Single-handing is thought by some to be unjustifiably risky. If I were lost at sea or forced to retire they would have faced heavy public criticism. Philip's faith in my ability to finish the event in one piece was difficult to ignore. Other people had worked tirelessly to make it possible for me to be in such a position. My thoughts turned to them and how they would feel about any suggestion of failure. Slowly I began to make the real commitment which the project had always demanded, I was over halfway and if I could just make the Cape of Good Hope, surely I could carry on.

From past experience I knew that no matter how much I might have convinced myself that it was impossible to go on, there would always be a niggling doubt about whether or not I could have continued. From here on I began to feel more intense about everything related to the success of the project. If anything, I started to drive harder to make up the time I was sure I would lose when either the pilots finally gave up or the fuel ran out.

The weather system we were in now was huge and seemed to extend right across to South Africa. The steady head wind did not give the windshifts that I relied on to allow fair progress. At first it had forced my track too far north and now I was heading south fast. Without wind shifts I had no control over my latitude whilst I chose to stay on favoured tacks. My resolve may have hardened but I felt totally drained from the work and the decision-making. I woke on the 18th aching and bruised with a fresh set of infected cuts from the struggle with the generator. But I had thought of some new ideas on how I might get this working and had one last stab at stripping it down. It was hopeless. I had to turn my attention now towards making the things that did still work last for the remaining distance.

I recalibrated the autopilot to be far less sensitive to being off course. This stopped the pilot motor from working excessively hard to maintain an accurate course. The boat would wander from side to side but maintain a fair average track. This both saved power and reduced wear on the mechanical parts of the pilot system, so I hoped it would allow me to stretch everything out just a little longer. There was no time to waste licking wounds, I had to start to make good miles and not allow the failures to slow us down. A fast passage would ultimately be more economical! The wind had eased right down, I was still too far north and was under the influence of the huge Indian

Ocean high pressure system. Feeling that I had made up my mind, I became more optimistic and started to push south again.

Despite being close to the high pressure it was still grey and bleak and very, very cold. The Henri Lloyd high-performance thermals and Ocean Racer foulies had been de rigueur. But now I was spending up to six hours helming a day and standing at the wheel it was easy to become numbingly cold with the relative inactivity. I also carried a Henri Lloyd SysstemAIR suit, a one-piece survival suit designed to give as much as three hours' survival time overboard as well as being a normal working suit. It achieves this with an inflatable double skinned liner which could be part inflated as I stood at the helm, providing a considerable improvement in insulation and warmth. Add to this, thermally lined mountaineering gloves and balaclava and I could extend my tolerance of the conditions on deck by many hours.

By 19th February (day 90) everything had taken on a very different feel. The new limit on power and pilot usage made the immediate future look bleak. I had become accustomed to the few luxuries that having virtually unlimited power afforded. The boat had seldom been quiet before, music or the radio were nearly always playing companionably and at night we were lit up like a Christmas tree because there had seemed no need to conserve power when the generator was running all night every night. Now the yacht was filled only with the noises of sails and water, while at night everything was done by torchlight or, if I was lucky, moonlight.

Telexes fired back and forth between Andrew Roberts and the boat as we tried to assess the best way to manage the remaining fuel and reduce consumption. As we communicated my gut feeling began to change from the gloom of potential failure to a feeling that I could eke out the fuel sufficiently to a point where the remaining distance without it would be one I could tackle without any power – just keeping enough back for the Channel and final approaches.

I reckoned I had been too pessimistic. Because I was still uncertain of the exact quantity of fuel remaining, I had erred heavily on the safe side when calculating this and I had also worked out where I could find small additional supplies in the sump of the tanks beyond the reach of the normal suction pumps. My moods changed as often as the weather, one moment I would feel confident and buoyant and the next uncertain and depressed.

I was becalmed totally during the night and, although I could have made a few miles using the pilot, I elected to furl sail and shut everything off, not wishing to use power for no real mileage gain. I left the main up and slept soundly on the saloon bench. Four hours later I was thrown to the floor when the wind picked up – the perfect alarm clock. It was very spooky with no lights, no wind and no sails, just the slapping of the swell – it was like sleeping on the *Marie Celeste*. I was gripped by a permanent, teeth-clenching tension, as I watched the fuel levels drop daily or listened to the noise of the pilot motor, just waiting for a failure. I kept finding new ways of saving power, like greasing the steering and slackening the cables to the wheel to reduce the friction in the system.

On the 20th a gentle north-easterly filled in and we were on our way again. The smooth seas allowed some rewarding sailing towards the Cape of Good Hope at last. Crossing the Southern Ocean was a bit like driving down a road with traffic lights every few hundred yards. I felt sure that if I could just make the Cape of Good Hope, I would know more exactly how much fuel I had used and would be able to tailor my decisions for the last few thousand miles.

I kept saying, 'These are easy miles and magic days,' but in reality I was finding it increasingly difficult to get out on deck and do the sail changes. Finding the motivation to get on with the job had become more difficult with the gear failure and lack of progress. The continual grind of the Southern Ocean was starting to wear me down. Before the generator failure I had been able to ignore the distance ahead. Now watching the 'distance to go' had become an all important part of everyday fuel calculations.

I had filled the diesel day tank (the only tank fitted with a sight gauge) when the generator failed. Now I was marking the side of the tank each day to assess how much fuel I was using. This was still complicated by the angle of heel but eventually I began to get a feel for how long each full tank would last. Early measurements showed that my worst estimate would allow three hours charging a day for a total of eight weeks and, based on current performance, I would still be at sea for a further twelve weeks. It was not encouraging. The thought of continuing without power was not so bad. I had a sextant and tables, and everything else simply made life easier. But without self-steering the boat was proving to be nearly impossible to manage. During a sail change *Group 4* would run off totally out of control. Everything was just too far away from the helm and I was constantly running back and forth trying to keep the boat tracking in a straight line. The answer was to heave to for each sail change but it was only a matter of time before something would go badly wrong.

Remembering Des Cooper's advice about eating properly, I baked some bread during the night and enjoyed the treat of beans on toast – maybe not haute cuisine but one of my favourites – for breakfast. I had now totally lost track of the menu system. Day by day, I just wandered forward and chose something different from the selection, trying not to choose my favourites every time, but there had to be some compensation for the increasingly uncomfortable conditions.

The next day, Monday 21st February, I sent a telex to Steve Moore at Autohelm to ask if it would be possible to lock the helm in any position using the broken pilot, hopefully using the power steer mode on the hand-held control for the infinite small adjustments needed to keep on track. The helm was lashed as much as possible now, but a method of quickly and accurately locking the helm, with the additional possibility of being able to re-trim it from below decks, would make things easier. He came back with a suggestion that I clamp off one of the hydraulic hoses to lock up the system, effectively jamming the helm. It had just one major disadvantage. To release the wheel I would physically need to remove the ram or release the clamp, which meant lifting the stern helmsman's seat off to gain access each time. It was not a significant improvement and for the time being I abandoned the idea, preferring to continue as I was. Both pilots still worked, but I realised I would need to save twenty-five per cent more fuel than my best efforts so far if I was going to keep power all the way home. The pilots are the biggest power user, and can double their consumption in severe conditions. Every day I could sail with the helm lashed would save fifty per cent of my normal fuel usage. I could run the boat for nearly two days on only three-hour charging at 1000 revs per minute.

At night it was cold, damp and dark down below. I curled up with my sleeping bag over my ears to shut out the solitary noise of clattering sails. Sir Alec Rose had advised Chay to carry candles on his voyage. I had scoffed at, but not ignored, the idea. Now I too watched the reflections of candlelight flickering off the dead high tech. screens in the nav. station. I had been sailing close to the rhumb line since things began to go wrong. Now I started to feel that I should cut every corner and started to track south towards the shorter Great Circle route in search of the quickest route.

On the morning of the 22nd I woke to find the lashing on the wheel had worked free, we had tracked off the wind and headed away from South Africa towards the south-east. I was furious that I had slept through the change but, with the pilot shut down, the alarm systems no longer functioned. I stomped about in a mood all morning. The lack of reliable alarms was to become an additional frustration. A telex came in during the two hours that I had the Inmarsat switched on. Andrew Roberts had completed the clinical tests and the results seemed encouraging as they indicated that by running the engine as I had been I should be able to stretch the remaining fuel supply all the way – just.

Then I saw the figures Andrew had based his calculations on and my heart sank, his estimates of my remaining fuel were far more optimistic than my own. I still appeared to be more than twenty per cent short. I telexed him back with the bad news.

A few hours later another telex from Andrew with a completely revised set of figures now showed I could still last all the way by using all the fuel in each tank sump. His telex ended with the immortal words, 'It's going to be tight.' I had to smile, if I had only a tenth of the fuel I had, I'm sure he would have been equally positive and it would have been equally 'tight'.

On the 23rd news reached me that the Challenge training yacht's mast had collapsed on a training sail off Plymouth. The bottlescrew on the aft lowers had failed whilst the yacht was beating to windward through heavy seas in the English Channel. *Group 4* was now pounding to windward through the Southern Ocean in near gale conditions, and the stresses placed on the rig as the boat plunged into each wave were enormous. Having had some experience of bottle-screw failures last time round, I felt a compulsive and immediate desire to inspect mine. So, despite the darkness and foul conditions, I crawled forwards with a torch through blinding spray and measured the threads for stretch or cracking. *Group 4*'s bottlescrews were okay and, I reminded myself, the bottlescrew on the training yacht had been a different design from those fitted to the ten Challenge yachts. There was no point in worrying but, on top of the other failures, it was an additional concern I really didn't need at the time. All the same, when daylight returned I fitted Spectra preventers to the two aft lowers, safety strops which would, I hoped, stop any catastrophic failure if a screw did break. They were really not needed but I would have been annoyed with myself if anything had failed and I had not taken the obvious preventative action.

As darkness returned with *Group 4* plunging south-west, the sky cleared after the passage of a cold front and the wind built to a full gale. As I began to furl the headsails, the sky exploded with Disney-like colours and the organ-pipe shapes of a full blown auroral display. The sky was filled with these most amazing, subtly changing colours and shapes for a full fifteen minutes, lighting up the rugged seascape with soft shades of red and green. I stood in the cockpit with my jaw hanging open. The aurora happens every night within roughly 1500 miles of both the North and South magnetic poles. *Group 4* was now moving rapidly towards the latter but this was to be the best display I had seen, for cloud cover normally prevents clear observation and each night only an eerie glow suggests its presence.

By the morning the seas had built to such an extent that, with the boat reefed down, we were not making good progress. I went up to try taking a reef out and found that a top batten had snapped and speared through the batten pocket. I dropped the main and ran off the wind, changing the batten and placing a sticky Dacron patch over the hole. In 35 knots of wind and with a steep sea running it was no easy job. Fortunately the sail itself was not pierced, only the pocket had failed. Back on the wind again progress was still frustratingly slow, the seas seemed far worse than those in the Pacific. Working at the mast in these conditions I would listen for the tell-tale hiss of breaking seas because moments later a wave would sweep the decks, plaster me up against the mast and leave me clinging on for dear life.

Worrying about the pilot and fuel started to affect everything I did. I even began to find it difficult to sleep whilst listening to the pilot motor winding back and forth. It seemed the heavy rolling of the yacht caused the pilot to work far too hard, as it tried to correct for every yaw the boat made. I had already detuned the settings and now I detuned them even further. Listening to the noise of the motor was like listening to a stopwatch ticking, counting down the remaining time I would have electricity and self-steering.

Group 4 slewed around under the new settings, trimming the boat helped, and after repeatedly trying different combinations, and then sitting in the cockpit to watch the outcome, I found that I could halve the power consumption as well as keep a fair overall course.

This was a plus. But to prevent me getting too optimistic, Autohelm sent bad news. I had been waiting for them to come up with a way of re-plumbing the electronics and hydraulics to avoid the need for the valves. I was sure they would come up with something but now sensed what they were reluctant to admit, that once the final two valves failed, this would mark the end of a workable pilot system. The news was bad, it seemed nothing could be done! I bitterly regretted my decision to put all my eggs in one basket with just one type of pilot system when one tiny hydraulic valve would shortly render it useless.

I had fleetingly considered fitting a windvane self-steering system, one that would not need power to operate, using a windvane to drive a steering rudder. But apart from the significant amount of work that would have been needed to modify the existing steering, it would have been exposed to breakage on the transom and the gears available were never designed to steer yachts the size and weight of *Group 4*. Ironically, of course, the loss of the pilot would have cured the fuel problem. Without the power consumption of the motors I would easily be able to stretch the fuel. I worked harder than ever, steering or lashing the wheel and only using the pilot when working on deck or when the wind drew aft of the beam.

The gales continued and on the 24th the barometer fell further. The seas went from plain rough, through frightening, to majestic. I dropped the main and continued under a part reefed staysail. *Group 4* actually went faster towards her destination without the mainsail in 45 knots of wind. Sitting more upright, leeway was less of a problem and the yacht tracked straighter.

The staysail sheet broke twice during the night, the sheets were so heavily loaded it was impossible to wind the sail in, even using the primary winch, and the holes in the alloy track which held the staysail cars were distorted by the morning. At dawn I was working at the mast, winding up the halyard tension when a loud bang sent the three-kilo bronze staysail car hurtling past my ear. The four turns of one-ton breaking strain sail ties used to prevent the cars from flying off had broken like thread. I lashed both cars in place with 12 mm line to keep them from flying off again. It is hard to describe the pressure the yacht was under in these conditions, but I refused to stop.

The wind was now straight out of the west, so progress was painful and slow. I headed south-west in the hope that I would find better wind angles underneath the Indian Ocean high pressure system, allowing us to sneak through without being becalmed for days on end or being hit by the more severe conditions further south. There seemed to be no compromise. Still the strong weather from the west allowed *Group 4* to progress across the chart with the helm lashed. I was constantly re-trimming the helm to stop the violent juddering of the yacht rounding up into the wind or, even worse, sailing off due north or south on a fast reach. It was frustrating but economical and I seemed to acquire a permanent headache which would not submit to pills.

On day 96, 25th February, we drew level with the bottom of the west coast of Australia, 4,500 miles of open ocean lay ahead. I was coming to terms with the changes that the gear failure had caused, and any temptation to retire to the safety of an Australian port lessened as we pulled out into the vast expanse of the Indian Ocean. That day, whilst going about in 35 knots of wind, I was shocked to watch the staysail suddenly fall to the deck, disappear over the side and fill with water, dragging behind the boat, held only by the sheet and foot. The stainless steel shackle at the head had shattered as the sail flogged through the tack. After retrieving the sail I began the tricky job of feeding the luff rope back into the foil groove and re-hoisting the sail on the pole lift halyard. The normal halyard being now stuck up the mast, it would need quieter weather before I could contemplate retrieving that. With the sail doing its best to fly away and waves rolling across the foredeck, the job proved difficult and dangerous. The luff rope was in good condition but the sail had chafed through where it passed each joint of the alloy foil. Hoisting it in these conditions could have torn the luff tape off completely. But with careful timing, and numerous ties to control the flogging, I eventually got the sail up, setting the halyard tension slightly tighter to reduce the load on the damaged luff tape.

I arrived below drenched with sweat, as I did now after any serious deckwork. Without heating the only way to dry clothes was to climb into a sleeping bag, fully dressed. During the night I was freezing, despite thermals and two good sleeping bags. It was colder now than it had been after Cape Horn. On the morning of the 26th a thin layer of ice made the cockpit and decks slippery and the vapour from my breath froze around my thermal balaclava. Light snow sprinkled the deck at midday as the wind began to ease down. By mid-afternoon I was becalmed in fog.

Since the failure of the generator, I had done little day to day maintainance, dealing with the bare essentials but no more. Now the boat was beginning to show signs of the continual pounding and the failure rate of deck gear had increased. I took the opportunity to carry out a full check, replacing the main halyard and both the staysail sheets, as well as reinforcing the preventers on all four deck cars. In addition I showered, cleaned the loos, pumped the bilges, soldered some torch terminals, cleaned the galley, reorganised the spares and tools, cleared out some unwanted food boxes, re-stowed some sails further aft, whipped some loose ends, washed some clothes and cleared the chart table out – anything to prevent myself from thinking about not moving in the calm.

I pushed still further south and by the following day had found the wind again. Weatherfaxes from Canberra showed just how close I had been to the centre of an enormous high pressure system that stretched from around 80° East to Tasmania. The sun came out for a few hours during the afternoon, for the first time for ten days. Soon a hard edged belt of fast moving low cloud swept in from the west, signalling a wind shift north-west and a sail change. Later the leech line in the yankee snapped, causing the leech of the sail to start motoring, the vibration reverberating through the hull as a constant reminder that the poor sail was flapping itself to bits. But after the previous day's calm I did not want to stop whilst I had a good breeze, so I pulled my spare sleeping bag over my head and slept.

During the night of day 99 the main engine refused to start, the batteries were flat. The main engine had always been very reliable and to my eternal relief it fired at the first turn of the key, once I switched all the boat's batteries towards starting it. It was the alternator which charged the engine batteries that had failed. From now on every time I ran the engine I needed to climb down and switch the batteries, so that they all charged from the other alternator. Each time I stopped the engine I had to remember to switch them back. The engine start batteries could not be allowed to run flat for the main engine was the only way of charging the battery banks. Without it I would have no power at all after three days' normal running, even with the economy measures.

The wind had now got up to 25 knots from the south-west and at last I headed straight towards the Cape of Good Hope at over 9 knots, a welcome change, even though I had to take the mainsail down later, as one of the batten cars had fallen off. The webbing strops that held the sail to the cars were starting to chafe through. The leech of the yankee continued to vibrate, but stopping to fix it was out of the question. *Group 4* was now on a roll and we were on our way to our last corner.

9

The Ocean I Love to Hate
(Day 100 – Day 121)

It was 1st March. One hundred days at sea had slipped past quickly, I had been worried that I might be affected by so much time alone. Now I began to worry that I was not! I celebrated our centenary with a large brandy from my Christmas barrel. Surely I had passed the depths. If I could just make the Cape I could make it back up the Atlantic – power or no power. By now my moods were totally governed by progress. When we were heading down the line, I felt great. Sure, there were problems but *Group 4* was still going and the Atlantic didn't seem so far away now. But if the weather was foul, so was my mood. I was convinced other things were going to fail and the success of the passage was anything but certain.

The wind eased down, the sky cleared and in the afternoon sun it was relatively warm. I took the opportunity to strip back the layers of thermals and damp clothes. In the evening the wind became light enough to take down the yankee and tackle the repair to the leech line. Not being able to tension the reproachfully flapping leech had been driving me nuts for the past two days. The leech line runs inside a pocket down from the head, round the clew, and back to the foot. Ideally, over a hundred feet of inaccessible 4 mm line needed replacing but drawing that much line through in one go would have been nigh impossible single-handed. Instead I made small incisions in the leech tape to gain access to the two broken ends and, drawing them together, stitched and seized the ends, then repaired each cut in the leech tape with small patches. The alloy jamming cleats that secured the line tension had both snapped in half, and the sail was badly cut up where the sharp ends had pierced it while flogging. I took them both off and tied the end of the line off. The damage needed several sheets of sticky Dacron to prevent it from getting worse. With the sail re-hoisted *Group 4* was under way again, the lack of vibration was wonderful, and my headache eased!

A new problem now presented itself with the steering. The compasses were becoming more and more sluggish as we neared the magnetic pole. I was forced to steer by keeping the wave patterns at the same relative angle or by heading towards a cloud formation, knocking the steering compass from time to time to free the card. Even the southern hemisphere compass, the one with a balanced card to compensate for the magnetic dip, was slow and equally unusable. The autopilot fluxgate caused the boat to veer around drunkenly, and alarms sounded frequently as the boat wandered off course. Several times I fell asleep at the wheel, waking only as the boat rounded up or dropped off the wind. I was doing the best I could to steer for more than six hours a day – sometimes in one hit or more frequently in shorter stints. Every moment I could steer now would improve the chance of success when the fuel ran out.

The following day the wind was still light, the seas had flattened out, but the never-ending swell remained. As I was now steering for long periods I missed the Windex wind indicator at the top of the mast. I had been promising myself to find a suitable moment to replace this ever since Cape Horn. For all the instruments and electronics, there is nothing like looking up the mast and being able to see a direct relationship between wind direction and heading. So I rigged the four-to-one purchase and, kitted out with the various tools and equipment, I began hauling myself aloft. It was slow hard work and I rested at each set of spreaders, tucking the excess line into a bag before I continued up. The gentle swell was greatly exaggerated at the top of the seventy-nine-foot mast and pulling a quarter of my body weight and preventing myself from slamming into the mast on each swing became increasingly difficult. It took twenty minutes to reach the limit of the block and tackle, just feet from the top, and I realised it was not going to be as simple as I had thought. The fitting which held the Windex in place was within reach, but it was going to be impossible for me to tighten the securing screw. I tried everything, including easing myself up in the chair and crouching precariously in the seat. Despite the low air temperature I was now dripping sweat and could feel the strength seeping from my hands and arms. I gave up, descending as quickly as I could. Back on deck, I shook with frustration and more than a little fear, abandoning any thought of a second attempt, and instead fitted the instrument back on the aerial mast on the stern where it had done duty since the Horn.

As it grew dark a thick bank of fog descended, wisps of vapour billowed down the companionway steps inside the boat. On deck the feeling of total isolation was completed by the dome of greyness that torchlight revealed. There was still very little wind and what there was shifted fast. The GPS showed that as much as 2 knots of current was setting me back to the east. Just to stay in the same place I would need to cover forty-eight miles a day. As I watched the plot move backwards down my track, it seemed to me that in calm weather the lack of surface turbulence allowed the current to accelerate. In rougher weather, when the slower moving deeper layers of water were mixing with the surface water, the current reduced.

The discomfort and continual grind of the Southern Ocean was eating away at my enthusiasm. Since the failure of the generator the day to day discipline that had kept me on top of the chores had faded. I knew I had made bad weather-routing decisions and sailed far too close to the Indian high pressure. My best hope now was the development of a small low to the north-west and I steered to meet its projected track. Thoughts of failure conspired with the bleakness of the place and I could feel myself slipping into a mire of self-pity again. I knew this was bad news and I tried to work through it, but even the most minor jobs became chores. The poor averages depressed me.

Soon I was reefing down again, the effects of the approaching weather system accelerated progress and *Group 4* charged forward at above 9 knots over a smooth swell. I was in the galley, making a flask of coffee, when I was shocked to hear a single long and very loud blast of a fog-horn. I raced on deck, which was fairly pointless as we were in fog so thick I could scarcely see the front of the boat. Rushing below again, I switched the radar on and waited nervously for the ninety-second warm-up period. A collision in such a remote place seemed inconceivable, but what I had heard was very close and very real. When the radar screen lit up I adjusted the sensitivity to maximum. Nothing was visible. Back on deck, I strained my ears for sounds of a ship's engines until finally I had to concede that I had imagined the sound. I worried about my sanity. If I had begun to hear things when I felt so normal, what would be next? Two hours later another loud blast made me realise what it was I had heard. The access holes in the side of the boom were acting like an orchestral wind section. The blast was nothing more than the wind blowing across the hole like an enormous flute. I might have developed a few idiosyncrasies, but inventing imaginary merchant fleets was not one of them – yet.

Short periods of calm interrupted the westerly breeze but on day 103 we were making fair progress again. The fog banks seemed endless. In comparison to the weather we had experienced here on the previous year's race, I was now recording day after day of direct head winds. The north-west/south-west wind shifts had not been either as regular or pronouced as I would have expected. After Tasmania I had been forced too far north and now, with long peroids of north-westerlies, I was heading too far south. The Kerguelen Islands were just to the south. I had reached the geographical halfway point and had again converged with our track of the previous year. I would now need to work harder than ever to use the weather systems to my advantage, finding the best wind direction which would allow me the freedom of the route choice as we approached South Africa.

The monotony of daily life was becoming harder to deal with. I wasn't lonely, I just felt bored. To make things worse I had read all my books at least once. It left me too much time to think. I began worrying about things at home again – the prospect of finishing the trip with all sorts of financial problems seemed so unfair. I knew this was ridiculous. I had been given the opportunity to take on the greatest challenge and was now allowing external problems to spoil the experience. It was just another effect of the continual grind and I longed for the optimistic trade-wind sailing days after the Cape of Good Hope.

On 5th March a steady rise in wind strength changed the scene around the boat again, bringing a return of steep breaking seas. It was in this area that the crews on the Challenge Race suffered the most severe injuries. The waves here followed no pattern and dropped on board from all angles, viciously and without warning. As I crawled forward I took extra care. By midday the wind was hitting 45 knots and I used the opportunity to film some spectacular waves crashing over the bows until, while at the mast, I was hit so hard by a wave it threw me to the end of my safety strop, knocking the breath from me as the chest harness jerked tight. Lying in the wash on the leeward side of the boat, still gripping the camera in one hand, I wondered at the sanity of trying to film, gave up and confined myself to essential work below decks.

The helm was still lashed and with the wind in the north-west *Group 4* was making good progress to the west. The boat was sailing herself well but I knew the pilot would have given her another knot or two of speed. Stretching the diesel and pilot relief valves into the Atlantic was essential and I knew it. In the trade winds *Group 4* would not steer herself downwind. The heavy angle of heel and exaggerated violent motion proved too much for the defunct generator. The rubber mounting feet broke, sending the whole thing crashing around loose in the wet locker, yet further evidence of the unit's unsuitability for the rigours of the Southern Ocean. The cooker hob jumped clear of its mountings again, this time along with a pan of spaghetti bolognese. After securing both hob and pans down with bungy cords, I slid around on hands and knees and started to clean up the disgusting mess on the floors and doors of the galley. Condensation streamed down all the bulkheads and mould had started to grow on the deckheads in the unventilated areas at the front and back of the boat. *Group 4* was starting to look how I felt.

Conditions became as bad as I had ever seen them by the following day. The wind was consistently over 40 knots and the seas were in the most evil mood since the gales after Cape Horn. I stopped using the loos, the risk of injury as the boat slammed off each wave was just too great. I made do with a bucket further aft instead and emptied it over the side. The wind shifted west and dropped for a short time, just long enough for me to replace a broken mainsail batten. As it gusted up again another 16 mm staysail sheet snapped with a sharp crack as the lazy end recoiled like a whip. I balanced on the rotating furling drum, trying to tie a new sheet on with one hand above my head and waves crashing around my waist. Hanging there above the deck on the inner forestay, with wild seas crashing underneath me, brought a manic smile to my face. I hated this place sometimes, but I was making progress through it – and I loved that!

The following morning, the third day of continuous gale-force winds, I celebrated the dawn with a Mars Bar and a hot cup of coffee (rather than the normal luke-warm cup from the thermos). Each hour during the night had represented another minor victory as the wind instruments recorded hour after hour of 40-knot winds, gusts occasionally reaching 55 knots. The strop which held the tack of the mainsail had to be changed each time I tacked the boat. The halyard tension needed to be so tight that the inboard end of the battens was being crushed if I forgot to change the tack strop before a tack. I rigged double sheets on the staysail and doubled the reefing pennants through the mainsail. *Group 4* was getting the severest test a sailing yacht can go through. Only my confidence in the yacht's ability enabled me to keep moving.

The forecast from Bracknell was not good, the weather was set to get even worse. I snugged the yacht down for more wind, lashing everything movable down. A short lull allowed me to sleep at the chart table as the light faded, but after an hour or so I woke with a start as the wind rose to 45 knots again. On deck the wheel lashing had worked free and the wheel spun wildly as *Group 4* found her own slot and continued to work her way through the blackness. I rigged with two harness strops and climbed on deck to retie the wheel. Even in the dark the scene was staggering, silhouettes of black mountainous seas surrounded the boat and horizontal spray filled the air, sparkling as it swept past the glare of the deck light. *Group 4* crashed from wave to wave, white water thundering over the decks with real ferocity. For a brief period the sky cleared and moonlight lit up the seascape, a view of turmoil to which no camera would ever do justice. I had experienced stronger winds after Cape Horn but somehow this seemed far more violent. I knew that the ocean acknowledged my passage no more than it would flotsam, but I still harboured a real feeling that it wanted to test us before we escaped to the relative safety of the Atlantic.

Dawn showed the whole picture. The view was magnificent. Huge rolling waves trundled towards *Group 4* in legions and, together with the low, fast-moving cloud, gave the impression that the world was in fast forward. The barometer hovered around 1000 mb and I prepared for it to turn either way. When the wind eased it held in the west, and progress through the aftermath of the gales was near impossible. I increased the sail area to try to power through the waves but until the seas reduced there was little point. Isolated squalls made it difficult to settle down to rest. I tacked back and forth in search of a favourable tack but, as usual, the wind had settled right on the nose. Fresh cuts on my hands, a lack of sleep, and the frustration of the lack of progress put me in an angry mood. I switched on the autopilot, as the wind was now too light to get the boat to steer herself through the huge seas. Then I climbed into my sleeping bag, pulling it over my head to shut out the stressful noises of *Group 4* struggling forward. Fifteen minutes later alarms sounded, indicating the port pilot relief valve had finally blown.

Despair took over. I felt convinced that this was the beginning of the end of the pilots. I switched on the starboard pilot (which I had been holding in reserve for the Atlantic), only to find that it, too, was indicating a fault. Using a small vice, I clamped the hose which runs into the broken valve, thus effectively rendering the valve shut, and locking the steering system. Then I altered the sail plan to enable us to track straight. Looking at the hydraulic system, with the clamp fitted to one of the pipes, I couldn't resist the temptation to engage the pilot motor. I hoped this might allow the system to work in some way. It certainly couldn't make things any worse now. It worked!

I shut it down, just in case it was going to do further damage, and contacted Steve Moore at Autohelm with a surprisingly good link made through Singapore Radio. It seemed such an obvious solution, and there was embarrassment on both sides as we realised that communication difficulties had prevented us from finding the solution earlier. This would allow the pilots to be kept working for the remainder of the passage. The only disadvantage was that when I wanted to take manual control of the steering wheel, I would need to remove the drive ram physically. I still had one good valve but could now keep this in reserve for the later parts of the voyage, where I would need the facility of regaining control of the wheel quickly.

Whilst I was sailing offshore a delay in regaining the wheel would be little more than an inconvenience. This discovery was like a breath of fresh air. In one hit fifty per cent of my troubles were cured.

The fuel shortage was now the major problem. With the pilots working again the increased power consumption would burn through the fuel more quickly, so I still needed to shut the pilot down as often as possible to save fuel. On the plus side, however, the fuel supply seemed to be holding out well. I had been more economical than we had thought possible. If I could arrive at the Cape of Good Hope with two tanks left, I felt sure I could stretch it out all the way home. A rare period of clear sky in the evening gave me a fine view of the aurora. I toasted my good fortune and slept soundly.

Heavy squalls and big wind shifts woke me at dawn on 9th March. The barometer was falling fast again and I was on deck in minutes, grappling with the mainsail. A petrel hovered a few feet away, eying me as if to say, 'What's all the fuss about?' Another series of gales swept towards us. But with just over 2,500 miles to the Cape and the prospect of some easier sailing and better weather ahead, my spirits lifted, despite the worsening conditions. I even seemed to be getting on top of the salt-water sores that plagued my wrists and neck. I had started to consume large quantities of Dextrose tablets, eating them like sweets during each sail change. As a result, many of the injuries seemed to clear up and in general I now felt fitter and more alert.

On the 11th nothing had changed. During the night I tried to reduce the continual slamming by steering further off the wind, which improved the angle at which we met each sea and the increase in speed more than compensated for the deviation from the required track. The wind speed wound up to a continuous 50 knots, with gusts of well over 60 knots. After so many days of storm-force winds I was getting nervous. I knew any serious problem on deck would be very hard to rectify in these conditions and as time went on my luck would eventually run out. When I made my way on to the deck I clipped on with two harness strops. Even so, I was getting increasingly scared each time I tried to do anything up there but hold on. Breaking seas would crash down, knocking me this way or that, trying to get me, I was convinced. To outwit them I would talk my way through even the smallest job, repeating over and over, 'I will not fall over the side,'

140

either in my head or out loud, anything to keep from losing concentration. I felt zombie-like and pumped even more Dextrose tablets to keep alert and awake. When I felt everything possible had been done, I went back to the nav. station for a frightening and sleepless night, made memorable by the incredible noise level as *Group 4* charged forward at 9 knots under staysail alone.

The following day as the wind eased, I gradually brought us back round on to course. I had made some useful northing, over eighty miles, and was confident that I was in the right place for some improved wind angles. The weatherfaxes showed cells of high pressure ballooning away from a large anticyclone under South Africa. To the north reports of two tropical cyclones indicated they would affect the area through which I would pass on my course towards the Cape. I spent the day clearing up and servicing winches, one of which had failed during the night, leaving me hanging on to the handle to prevent the staysail sheet from firing off the drum. The immediate forecast from Bracknell looked more settled and I relaxed and slept. In the evening I tried to contact Group 4 HQ at Broadway, but the radio was useless, white noise blocked everything. In the hour I spent trying to make the link the weather deteriorated again. The familiar sequence began once more and within a few hours the boat was struggling forward in 50 knots of wind.

Next morning the wind shifted south and I began clearing up the mess. Locker doors were hanging off yet again, even the loo two seats which had been flapping up and down like castanets had broken from the slamming. On deck it took several hours to tidy the cat's cradle of lines that the night had left. The feeder arm for the staysail had snapped and the halyard needed replacing. But at last I was able to head down the track towards South Africa with a fair wind. Hundreds of birds, mostly petrels, gathered around the boat during the afternoon of the 13th, with the Kerguelen Islands just to the south, then just as quickly, they disappeared again. I tried to catch up on sleep but the fickle head winds returned within hours. I tried to stay on top of them, tacking on each shift, but I was now very tired after all the bad weather and this was frustrating and testing work. I moved about in a dreamlike state, doing half one job then half another. It was a dangerous condition to be in and I knew it. To make matters worse

I became ill. The food should all have been sterile, so I put this down to a general lack of housekeeping in the galley and set penitentially about cleaning everything with sterilising solution – now was no time to get sick.

By the morning of 15th March things began to look up. I felt better generally, the sun was out and, with a gentle breeze from the east, we made fair progress under a light spinnaker. The afternoon sun was warm and, peeling off layers of thermals I slowly worked through some checks and maintenance. The light spinnaker had needed repairing and I was puzzled as to how it had got damaged. I found the rather obscure answer in the forepeak where the sail is normally stowed. The anchor box, containing a 135-pound CQR anchor and 200 foot of heavy chain, had broken free during the last gale and the four one-inch-thick teak corner pieces had split from top to bottom, exposing sharp screw tips. The whole lot had to be hauled out and I embarked on some schoolboy carpentry as I screwed, glued, clamped and, just for good measure, lashed the box back together again.

A high pressure ridge was developing to the south so I gybed to the north in search of more wind. Apart from perhaps avoiding a gale or two at around the longitude of Cape Leeuwin I did not think my northerly track had paid off so far. Now I felt sure that, with tropical cyclone Litanne affecting the weather to the north and the high pressure system to the south, I was about to get a large and overdue pay-off. In the evening a spectacular Dante's Inferno-red sky and crescent moon made the day a memorable one. The prospect of better weather, more favourable winds and, above all, arriving back in Atlantic waters was cheering. Smells of fresh bread filled the boat and I sat in the cockpit with a beer in one hand, book in the other till the light faded, a wonderful change.

With 1,650 nautical miles to go to the Cape the favourable winds came and went, calms and shifting winds infuriated and frustrated me, but progress was improving. The Cape of Good Hope is almost as notorious as Cape Horn and I worried about what it might hold. *Group 4* had come through some severe weather, but each time I was left with the feeling that if the Southern Ocean had so chosen, it could have been much, much worse. I had experienced winds of up to 60 knots – what would winds of more than a 100 knots do? It hardly bore thinking about, but this ocean, more than any other, is capable of producing such weather. Strong currents still slowed us but, despite periods of calm, things continued to improve. I was feeling more and more confident about fuel. The strict economy measures were paying off. With the jury-rigged autopilot working well the steering system no longer seemed to be a major problem. Apart from the relief valves, the pilot had been very reliable, and I carried spares for all the other components.

A bank of fog was turned pink by a red sunrise on the 17th and a calm gave way to a teeth-clenching charge towards the Cape. The clamped pilot worried me in these conditions. If *Group 4* broached badly I would be unable to regain the helm quickly enough to prevent a knock down. At night this was especially worrying. As during the storms, I sat at the top of the companionway steps, half asleep, manually correcting the pilot system when it was a little late or slow in correcting the helm. Running at breakneck speeds is far more stressful than upwind sailing in some ways. The real risks are more concealed because the apparent wind is so much lower than it really is and it is far too easy to get caught with too much sail set. Upwind an increase in wind speed can be felt much sooner. Apart from the steep angle of heel, the increase in noise below decks warns of the need to reef down. The Southern Ocean is a very different beast for a yacht travelling westabout. The weather systems which cross the ocean heading east or south-east travel at around 30 knots, a yacht travelling with them at 10–15 knots has the advantage that each system's closure speed is as low as 15 knots. A yacht travelling westabout, against the prevailing conditions, not only has to over-come as much as 2 knots of current, but each system closes at over 40 knots. The result is more frequent changes of wind speed and direction, therefore more deckwork.

My average since Tasmania had been more than a knot less than the fully crewed times and, although I had never expected to be anywhere near as fast, still I found this disappointing. It was a larger deficit than on any other stage so far. Now I was going to use this downwind opportunity really to push *Group 4* hard.

On the 19th we were still flying. At last the daily mileages were reaching 220 nautical miles or more. The occasional squall made holding the spinnaker distinctly borderline, but I work on the principle that God would take it down if he so wanted. The seas had picked up from the south-east now and, with a swell still running from the west, *Group 4* would occasionally pile straight through an exceptional sea. Working at the mast required more care than ever, the easier motion was deceptively dangerous.

Radio communication had been almost impossible for the past two weeks. The telex at Group 4 control had been out of action for a few hours, so I made a concerted effort to establish a radio link. I wanted an up to date weather report, knowing that, if I could get the next few days right, I might carry the fair wind all the way to South Africa. As I spoke with Charles Rice at Broadway the wind suddenly shifted south. I altered course from the nav. station, heading the boat further off the wind whilst I finished the call.

On deck I set about getting the spinnaker down, as by now it was blowing over 28 knots from the south. I released the guy which normally collapses the sail behind the mainsail and went forward to pull down the sock, but the line was jammed in the pulley block at the top of the mast. Now I had a serious problem, with near 3,700 square feet of sail and a strong breeze, it would be impossible to recover it without the squeezer. Suddenly, a stronger gust hit and the spinnaker wrapped around both the forestay at the top and the inner forestay at the bottom, two huge tightening twisted balloons of cloth. Making matters worst, the sock control lines, still my main hope of recovering the sail, were now firmly twisted into the wrap. It took me three hours, well into the night, of foot by foot tugging, twisting, winching and seizing before I finally had the flailing sail down in the safety of the forepeak, undamaged but a tangled mess of twists and sail ties. The saving grace had been the two furled headsails which hadn't allowed the wrap to get as tight as a bare stay would have. I was also able to unwind the wrap from the deck by rotating the furling drums. Very much relieved, I set a poled out yankee and brought the boat back on track, then collapsed in the saloon and slept.

I was woken during the night as *Group 4* was screamed along at 14 knots through the pitch black, vibrating the hull but perfectly balanced and glued on to the back of a wave moving at the same speed. We must have ridden it for near five minutes, with great

Above, crashed out in the saloon between emergencies. Below, regular Southern Ocean windward work.

Above, rendezvous off the south Tasmanian coast. Below, a big forty-foot roller about to sweep the boat. As on the Challenge Race, the Indian Ocean was to prove the most testing stretch of the Southern Ocean.

Above, unusually clear skies in Southern Ocean latitudes, and everything going well - but not, alas, in the right direction as we are forced to beat off course. Below, sailing westward at last into the sunset, a beautiful feeling.

Group 4 off the Cape of Good Hope and pointing home.

Above, the South Atlantic proved it could be just as rough and unpredictable as anywhere else. Below, ideal trade wind sailing.

Above, the taunting oily calm of the doldrums. Left, a rather disorientated land bird visitor off the coast of Brazil. Below, dolphins were frequent and welcome visitors on the Atlantic legs and much missed in the Southern Ocean.

Above, a triumphant return past the Needles grinds to a halt, below left, on the Shingles when there is more tide than breeze. 'Why don't you start the engine?' someone suggested helpfully. Eventually, we got off in the early evening, below right.

Group 4 had proved her mettle - and her metal - by sailing westabout round the world in 167 days, 7 hours, 42 minutes and 54 seconds, beating Chay's record by 125 days, and justifying the faith placed in the project by Jørgen Philip-Sørensen who, with Chay, came aboard in Southampton to present me with the Global Challenge Trophy.

explosions of bioluminescence in the bow wave and a broad milky wake extending back as far as the waves would allow me to see. The following morning the wind eased and the seas became more reasonable. I re-hoisted the heavy spinnaker, carefully inspecting each section as it popped open, and relieved find only the sock itself looked any the worse for wear.

I had moved north out of the roaring forties. Fair-weather cumulus and sunshine made a pleasant change from the usual gloom. The remnants of ex-tropical cyclone Litanne were still serving us well and I tried to push further north to keep the breeze as long as possible. The spinnaker sock jammed again the next day as I was dropping the sail for a gybe and I had to go through the entire rescue procedure once more. I racked my brains for what was different. Up until now I had dropped the spinnakers time and time again without a real problem, so why had I started hitting problems every time? It was moments like this, I thought ruefully, that highlighted the fact *Group 4* was never designed as a solo boat.

Next day frustrating wind shifts returned with a vengeance. I did my best to keep my cool but by midday, having gybed through every shift, I was exhausted. I steered for an hour, then watched for an hour. With no change in the wind, I gybed north-west, chanting my mantras during the gybe and watching as my speed over the ground was reduced to just 4 knots with 3 knots of current running south-east. This gybe was unfavoured due to the strong current, but the favourable Agulhas Current was now only a few hundred miles away. By pressing north I hoped to find it sooner.

What I found first was another unopened Christmas present, a barrel of brandy, in the cornflakes locker, which literally had hidden depths and kept producing lucky dip surprises. It certainly helped cheer me up on what had become another depressing day's progress. We were sailing well enough, but the current just reduced progress to what felt like a near standstill.

By the 22nd the sea temperature had risen four degrees, the current was still against us, but all the signs were for an improvement. The weatherfaxes indicated light airs ahead, and I was determined to get out of this foul current before the strong wind eased. In the evening, I saw the first sea life since Tasmania – rather surprisingly, a flying fish.

More than 6,000 miles of Southern Ocean, famed for its marine mammal life, had passed under the keel without my seeing a single whale or dolphin. I found this astonishing and worrying.

I started to put away the charts for the Southern Ocean and organise the ones for the Atlantic. With the trade winds so close now, I serviced all the spinnaker running gear, cutting back the chafed guy ends and filing down all the snap shackle hinges to prevent them from jamming. The hazy blood red sunset was distinctly different from those of the open ocean. Africa was close, I could feel it. The night began crystal clear with a new moon over where Africa should be. The Southern Cross lay astern. It was a very different night to those of the past month. I sat in the cockpit and marvelled at the prospect of getting out of the Southern Ocean safely. The forecast even indicated that the fearsome Cape of Good Hope would be in a mild mood. The Indian Ocean had again proved to be the toughest and most testing stage of the Southern Ocean. It's a place I love to hate! When things were bad the feeling of impending failure had been much stronger, now I started to feel more positive about everything. I knew I could finish but knew too I could not afford to relax until I was sailing into the Solent.

As if to confirm this, a bank of cloud swept in and flickering balls of lightning lit the cloud like a fluorescent tube. As I watched, the current that had been working against me stopped within a half hour. I had reached the Agulhas Current. The change from the cold Southern Ocean Current to the warm was dramatic and the swells and waves produced by a modest wind gave truth to the stories of great ships foundering here in record waves. The sea itself looked gobsmacked by the change of current, heaving up and down in great directionless mountains. Soon the lightning drifted astern and the GPS began to show a favourable current building.

At dawn the change was further marked by the appearance of sea life, as first pilot whales and later dolphins surrounded the boat. Although I had still not rounded the Cape, I felt a great weight lifting from me. I was back in the land of the living.

10

Knock Down
(Day 122 – Day 139)

Group 4 now had the bit between her teeth. With the favourable current we averaged over 14 knots during the early morning of 23rd March, surfing through huge swells. As I worked my way forward to gybe the spinnaker, steep waves occasionally broke heavily over the bows. Even with the spinnaker squeezed, the foredeck was a risky place in these conditions. But the exaggerated techniques for survival which the Southern Ocean had taught me were now instinctive and I continued to move in a slow measured way as I worked on deck, crouched down to prevent an accidental fall and doing nothing that I could not get out of, double-checking everything before proceeding with a reef or a spinnaker drop. One mistake could still mean at best the loss of a critical sail or damage to its gear, at worst a bad injury or man overboard. So the mantras remained a part of every piece of foredeck work.

A Westland petrel that was easily identifiable due to a missing flight feather had been with the boat for the past week, following our wake during the day and mysteriously disappearing each night. I unimaginatively named him Broken Wing and was used to him being around. On the 24th as *Group 4* made the final approach to Cape Agulhas, dolphins followed us towards the Atlantic. Broken Wing was so shocked when a dolphin leapt into his sea-skimming flight path that, in an effort to avoid a collision, he crashed into the back of a wave, a ball of feathers and legs splayed everywhere. It was as poor display of flight reaction as you would ever expect to see in a seabird

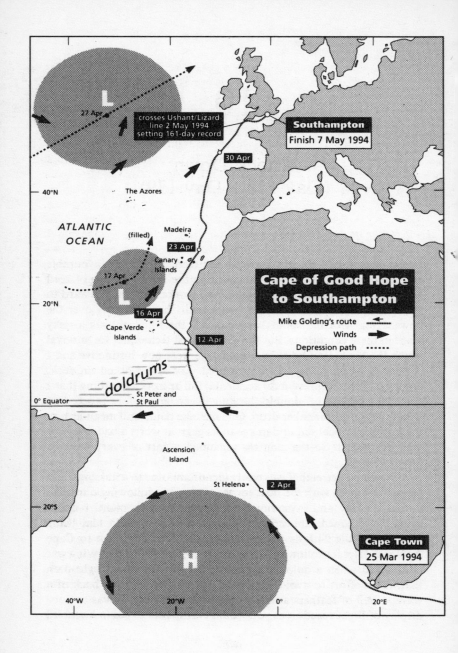

Cape of Good Hope to Southampton

Mike Golding's route ················
Winds ➤
Depression path ·······

crosses Ushant/Lizard line 2 May 1994 setting 161-day record

Southampton
Finish 7 May 1994

27 Apr

40°N

The Azores

ATLANTIC OCEAN

(filled)

Madeira

23 Apr

17 Apr

Canary Islands

20°N

16 Apr

Cape Verde Islands

12 Apr

doldrums

St Peter and St Paul

0° Equator

Ascension Island

St Helena

2 Apr

20°S

H

Cape Town
25 Mar 1994

30 Apr

L

L

40°W   20°W   0°   20°E

and probably an example of how he got his broken wing. I was mean enough to crease up with laughter. It was so strange to see a seabird actually screw up – they are normally such terrible aerial show-offs. I saw him later, looking fine, but perhaps flying just a smidgen higher.

The wind became cyclonic, eventually falling calm, and I caught up on sleep whilst waiting for the breeze to return. After a few hours I woke when a light southerly picked up. In the evening I saw the first ship since Tasmania, or rather two ships, a tug towing a large coaster with an enormous hole straight through the bow section. I tried to call them up to find out what had happened but they did not respond. Chay had a novel method of alerting any ship that passed too close. He put up warning explosives to attract their attention. You may well have been able to get away with that during the 'seventies, but if one went around lobbing sticks of dynamite at ships in the 'nineties, someone could get pretty upset. For my part, I kept look out during the night, preferring to save the battery power the navigation lights would use.

The high average speeds of the past week brought the overall Southern Ocean average up by 0.3 knots. So I now began to worry again that I might need either to ease up or, worse, stop to make the Cape Town rendezvous. The film crew, I knew, had been caught out by my acceleration and were scrabbling to be in place in time. I was relieved when I heard they had landed in Cape Town and were preparing to leave in a high-speed powerboat for an early morning filming rendezvous.

A long night dodging shipping was followed by a grey dawn and the first sight of land since Tasmania. The rugged coastline of South Africa was a welcome sight, arriving with an overcast dawn on 25th March. I finally made the first major alteration to the north, another nautical milestone in *Group 4's* progress as we surfed north-west up the coast at 10 knots, heading for the penultimate rendezvous. Seals and dolphins played round the boat as the coastline slipped quickly past and after a few hours we sailed out of the overcast weather and into a beautiful day with the memorable sight of Cape Point and the Cape of Good Hope, now just a few miles away, and the staggering outline of Table Mountain rising ahead.

A swish James Bond-style motor yacht, with the rather unbecoming name *Scuttlebug*, appeared. Moments later a helicopter converged on us with precison timing. *Group 4* surfing past the infamous Cape must have made a fine sight, for conditions were near perfect, with bright sun reflecting off the sea in a spectacular way. After an hour of being chased down the coast towards Cape Town, I could feel the wind easing and, not wishing to get caught in the Parking Lot as the area in the lee of Table Mountain is known, I gybed the spinnaker and started to head offshore again. The rendezvous – the handing over of film and an interview with Judy Hill of the BBC – took place in mid-gybe, before I re-hoisted the spinnaker, and so caused the minimum hold up. The wind freshened as Table Mountain steadily receded into the afternoon haze, and the most successful, certainly the most efficient, rendezvous was all but over. Perhaps we were all getting better at it? I never could make up my mind what I felt about these scheduled contacts with the outside world. I knew they were essential PR for Group 4 and they offered me a datum point from which to measure performance. I always looked forward actually to seeing fellow human beings but, when it came to the crunch, I hated the thought of being delayed and losing time. My obsession with forward progress down the track was all-consuming. *Scuttlebug* did a quick pass just ahead and, with the crew waving farewell, made a course back towards the coast. I was alone once more. I had already had one beer too many during the day, now I threw the last vestiges of caution to the 20-knot wind and opened yet another. I had drunk more than a week's ration in one hit and, with the accumulated lack of sleep, I was soon oblivious in the saloon. When I woke with a sore head and a dry mouth it was getting dark. I turned the nav. lights on and retreated to sleep out my hangover. It was good to be back in the Atlantic.

As if to remind me that there was still a long way to go, the starboard pilot started to play up again next afternoon. It indicated that the batteries were low – which they were not – and would not engage. I adjusted the computer and all was well again. Two days after the Cape rendezvous the weather was as frustrating as ever. Light airs from astern shifted back and forth, no sooner had I gybed than they would shift again. It was back to work as usual. I experimented with leaving the lazy pole rigged, rather than re-stowing it on deck, to save having to unship it each time. But this only added to the chaos of poles, sheets, guys and sails on deck during any gybe or sail change and I gave it up as one of my less good ideas. My best time for a gybe was seventeen minutes, and my worst more than two hours. It was hot now and each manoeuvre had me sweating heavily.

It wasn't just the sailing that was frustrating, the light spinnaker was nearing the end of its useful life. It was now on its second trip around the world and the cloth was like tissue paper. I took it down twice during the day to put a total of eight patch repairs on it. Then I went up the mast to tape up an exposed split pin, the cause of the spinnaker damage. The autopilot control unit in the cockpit gave up and needed exchanging, and finally the watermaker filters blocked and needed replacing.

But by the evening, when I sat in the cockpit watching the sun drop into the sea, with a large whisky and strains of Pachelbel wafting out from below decks, I knew this was the start of the trades. Under a huge full moon low on the horizon and scudding clouds from the south, we started to fly. Short breaking seas chased *Group 4*'s stern in a vee formation, great arcs of thundering water sheering up on each side of the bows as we hit speeds of up to 15 knots. Down below the deep vibration and the rising noise of the hull resonating warned me as the wind reached the practical limit of flying a spinnaker solo. I changed to a poled out yankee and started to reef the mainsail as the wind touched gale force. It felt as though I was standing on a giant surfboard, surfing an endless wave through a moonlit seascape. The motion was smooth with tremendous surges of speed and noise, but the occasional violent broach was uncomfortable and probably felt worse than it really was for, with the pole set high and the boom deliberately jacked up at a steep angle, we were in no immediate danger of digging any spars in. But a further reef in the mainsail and a big chunk of headsail wound away brought more control back, with little loss of speed.

Admiralty Sailing Directions recommend crossing the equator and the doldrums a long way to the west of a direct route, and many more up to date sources also offered the same advice, as the doldrums belt is statistically thinner to the west. But on the Challenge Race many boats found success sailing a more direct route, bucking established thinking, whilst those a little further west suffered longer delays. None of the Challenge boats chose to risk sailing the extra miles of the traditional route. The information in the Admiralty Sailing Directions is often old, some is even collated from reports from square-rigged ships of the 1800s. It does not take into account the windward and light airs performance of modern sailing yachts. So I planned my own route, electing to try for one close in to the African coast.

For three days the strong trades held steady and *Group 4* was eating up the miles. Occasionally I would need to gybe, but generally it was easy and relaxing sailing with bright sun, blue seas and flying fish leaping away from either side of the bows. This was what I had been waiting for, perfect conditions for winding down after the Southern Ocean. I slept, read and relaxed out on deck, finally free of the heavy thermals and foul-weather clothing. The nights were cool and watching the miles counting down every day was marvellous.

I cleared out surplus and out of date food, ditching it over the side. Keeping the boat's weight down had always been a fascination. Now, with the doldrums ahead, it was time to get the boat as light as possible to help keep moving when the wind dropped. Although I was now months ahead of Chay, I still felt that it was absolutely essential to finish as fast as possible. I was still racing the next challenger and I drove the boat as hard as ever – something which has always been my favourite pastime and was an essential part of my daily motivation. I wanted to make life for the next challenger as difficult as possible.

On the last day of March squalls, wild wind shifts and changes in speed kept me busy again, gybing back and forth, then eventually dropping the spinnaker and running with a poled out yankee as the wind began to exceed 30 knots. At daybreak a slight wind change forced another gybe but allowed me to re-hoist the 2.2-ounce spinnaker. However, the wind would not settle. Half the time the spinnaker barely defied gravity and the next moment we were overpowered and broaching out of control as the autopilot struggled to recalibrate itself for the change of conditions. The cause of all this were banks of black cloud with rain clearly visible beneath which now surrounded the boat. These clouds are best avoided if possible, as the squalls beneath them affect progress for an hour or more, initially with a burst of speed, then a big wind shift and finally with a period of light airs before eventually getting back to the normal gradient wind. With a full crew they can be used, but solo they are just a pain in the neck.

The Southern Ocean had provided a day by day challenge but now in these easier conditions, I was missing the competition of other boats more than ever. I really just wanted to get home now and in the slack moments needed to guard against dangerous complacency or carelessness. For example, I had just let the spinnaker squeezer bucket swing into my back, bruising it and my ribs quite painfully. I would never have let that happen in the Southern Ocean.

On 1st April strong squalls kept things busy. I dressed and prepared to drop the heavy spinnaker time and again, but on each occasion the wind eased down before I actually got around to dropping the sail. In the end I helmed during the stronger conditions and moved as much weight as I could towards the stern to help the autopilot keep control when I needed to rest. It was exciting sailing, with the boat averaging more than 11 knots. Surfing off each wave would occasionally drive the bows into the back of the sea ahead, scooping blue water up over the bows and through towards the cockpit in a foaming mass. Most of the time the autopilot could cope, applying lots of helm to prevent a violent broach, but occasionally it was not quick enough to prevent *Group 4* from laying over, trailing the boom through the water, with the spinnaker flogging violently as I scrabbled to release the pilot ram and bring the boat back on to track. There was no real need to push hard, but this was fantastic sailing, great progress and I loved it.

News came in on the Inmarsat that *Enza* had finished at the Ushant/Lizard finish line in the amazing time of seventy-four days. It seemed like a long time had passed since we had crossed tracks in the Southern Ocean. After the generator failure I had not been able to afford the power to contact them again. They faced some of the worst conditions of the whole circumnavigation in their final twenty-four hours, eventually surfing across the finish line with no sail up and towing warps to maintain control. It was a stark reminder that the Atlantic could be as bad as anywhere else in the world.

St Helena was only a hundred miles to port on day 132, and I was able to chat with Alan, the island radio operator. He made it sound an idyllic place, somewhere I would love to visit some day, full of history as the scene of the Emperor Napoleon's exile and death, and one of the last Atlantic islands not spoiled by an airport, relying solely on a twice monthly shipping service. With just 6,000 inhabitants everyone knew everyone, Alan explained, which made crime a rarity. He told me about a recent burglar who had broken in through the roof of a house, but before leaving had tidied the place up after him and carefully replaced all the roof tiles before making off.

The wind eased during the early morning on day 133 and I slept well, being disturbed twice for minor wind shifts. In the morning it was obviously going to be a superb day so I had breakfast up in the cockpit.

The short periods of sleep, never more than two hours in one hit, and the cold of the Southern Ocean, meant that I consumed an awful lot of hot drinks, and I had now finally run out of coffee, having drunk my way through five large drums. Opening the parcel marked for Easter, I was pleased to find 400 cigarettes (which I wasn't yet short of), a half dozen chocolate eggs and a *Mayfair* magazine which I read cover to cover in the same time it took me to eat the eggs. My relaxed start to the day was interrupted when I noticed that the spinnaker had split a couple of feet across the central seam. I was amazed it hadn't just blown out and quickly got it down to repair what turned out to be chafed stitching from the continual rubbing on the forestay. The final routing chart was now out on the chart table and each time I went below, my eyes would be magnetised towards the top right-hand corner where the UK was just visible. At last the finish was really in sight. I had stopped worrying about the fuel supply, the autopilots were working well now, I was running the jury-rigged pilot almost continuously and, though the ram developed a nasty rattle, it kept working.

On 4th April I woke with a start. The boat was juddering violently. It was 0240 and something had gone badly wrong. I swung out of my bunk and headed toward the cockpit, a second even more violent judder caused me to grab the edge of the chart table to prevent a fall. Thoughts of a lost rig or collision with a ship flashed across my mind. The violence of the motion in an otherwise smooth sea was terrifying.

On deck it was a pitch black moonless night. A scan across the deck with a torch revealed nothing and I rigged the searchlight to have a better look. Everything appeared fine, the spinnaker was drawing and all its gear was intact. If *Group 4* had just been shaken once, I would have said that perhaps we had hit a part-submerged barrel or glanced off a rogue container but the second hit, and the time delay between, was inexplicable – unless . . . It started to occur that we might have hit a whale, or a whale had been inspecting *Group 4*.

I must admit to having previously scoffed at most stories like this. How could a whale, equipped with such a vast array of natural senses, some of which we don't even begin to understand, allow a boat just to run into it, or mistake a boat for something living and threatening? It just seemed too far fetched. All the same, not taking any risks, I inspected the bilges, checked the steering gear and ran the main engine, sweeping the searchlight around for a few minutes to scare any other whales off. I was very glad to be in a steel boat and within an hour I was back in my bunk dreaming vivid dreams of sea monsters and sinking yachts.

When I woke it was another blisteringly hot day. More spinnaker repairs kept me busy. The light spinnaker seemed to be deteriorating badly with ultra-violet damage and every day I could prevent a complete blow out was now a bonus. The quiet days were allowing almost too much time to think, either lying on deck at night looking up at the vastness of the universe and thinking this cannot all be for our benefit, or contemplating the vast depths that *Group 4* had crossed. Really very little is known about the deep oceans, which cover seventy per cent of the earth's surface. On average there is about four kilometres of water beneath a boat sailing in mid-ocean. Incidents like the collision with something unknown reaffirmed the fact that, although the surface may seem lifeless and empty, beneath the keel life and death dramas are occurring at every moment.

Both day and night, it was uncomfortably warm now. I could only get to sleep lying out on deck where the breeze kept me cool. Waking with a full canopy of stars above was wonderful, the kind of experience you read about but never quite find the conditions to enjoy for yourself. I was waiting for the trades to fade. The light airs of the doldrums were just ahead. The weatherfax showed very few isobars in the waters I would reach in just a few days. The winds eased but kept blowing and *Group 4* continued to clock 200-mile days under glorious clear skies and through azure seas. Shoals of flying fish leapt away from the bows like starlings, flying formation for several

155

hundred yards before, as a group, disappearing back across the air/sea boundary into their other world.

The following day I was busy answering radio enquiries about the collision, but between calls I kept hearing a familiar and distinctive female Scottish voice talking to her boyfriend on a survey ship working off the coast of Africa. When I heard the name Playfair I was certain that it was the voice of an old friend, Susan Playfair whom I had met in the Shetlands during the Round Britain and Ireland Race. Portishead obligingly put me through for a good long chat. I was a little worried about what the boyfriend might think if he was still listening to the open circuit, but at least he couldn't come after me with his survey ship. Listening in to others' radio calls becomes a regular pastime for long-distance sailors. Wives, far from telling their husbands how much they are missed, usually provide endless lists of things that have gone wrong in the house or with the car – it's amazing how many sailors' cars seem to get crashed whilst they are away at sea – and there are always bills to be paid as the pay cheque never arrives on time. All the calls finish with quick 'I love you's and, duty done, relieved-sounding sailors go back to their work.

The doldrums conditions arrived with a bang on 7th April. The result was a shredded spinnaker, a smashed spinnaker pole and other minor damage. At 0315 hours *Group 4* was sailing smoothly in little more than 12-knots of wind, and I was in the saloon working the weatherfax when the wind-shift alarm signalled the start of an exceptionally busy night. I casually wandered up to re-trim the sails, as I had done several times in the hours before but, in what seemed like seconds, the entire vista changed from the serenity of trade-wind sailing to the fury of a bad doldrums thunder squall. Rain, thunder and lightning erupted and in moments the spinnaker was overpowering the boat and, like a toy, we were laid firmly on our side, with the spinnaker flailing but holding us over. The wind must have exceeded gale force, though I can't say I looked. Water was in imminent danger of pouring through the off-centre hatches which were open for ventilation. Having few choices I opted to release the spinnaker guy and with a terrific noise the guy almost smoked off the winch and out through the block with a whip-like action. The 16 mm pole preventer which is supposed to stop the pole from hitting the forestay failed and the full force of the overloaded sail smashed the pole into the forestay, snapping it in two like matchwood.

The jagged alloy edges of the pole flailed around fifteen feet off the deck and were in danger of tearing the spinnaker or, even worse, the headsail. With the boat upright and screaming downwind in torrential rain, I struggled in my underpants in the dim deck lights to get the spinnaker and pole down before the sail was damaged, but there was little hope of total success and in seconds the writhing spinnaker was ripped apart.

With the shredded spinnaker eventually under control, the clearing up began. The deck was a disaster, the stanchions and guard wires had been smashed inwards by the highly loaded guy, the pole was smashed and wrapped around the forestay, the tube in two, but the various control lines held the pieces vaguely together like tendons. Other lines were trailing behind the boat. Below decks, rain and waves had poured into open hatches and my relaxed trade-winds stowage arrangement found the floor strewn with soggy books, clothes, food and galley equipment.

Two hours later and with the wind back down to 12 knots *Group 4* was sailing again, now with the asymmetric spinnaker set on the port pole. The loss of the pole and sail was annoying, as from now on I would need to manhandle the pole across the boat, working it through the inner forestay and babystay on each gybe. The heavy spinnaker had been a very useful sail, covering a wide range of conditions, but the asymmetric was a fair replacement in terms of area and I doubted we would lose any serious time. This squall had caught me completely unawares. Threatening clouds had been around all day but none had produced anything like that and now the gentle south-easterly wind seemed as steady as ever. But I remained on the alert, running on deck whenever the wind-shift alarm sounded.

I crossed the equator without great ceremony on day 139, and within hours began to see more regular shipping traffic. These were the first vessels since the Cape of Good Hope and a sure sign that I was now approaching the busier northern hemisphere. I toasted Neptune for the fourth time in two years. Cloud banks were all around, but none produced squalls. However, since the knock down I had become reluctant to fly the light spinnaker. Then in the evening of the 10th it seemed so settled again, I decided to give it a go. When it was set it added another half a knot of boat speed and was more forgiving to trim.

There was abundant sea life everywhere now. Schools of dolphins worked to round up tuna, and only half a mile away whales leapt fully clear of the surface, crashing back with tremendous explosions of white water. Every visit on deck revealed a new sight. Below deck had another novelty to offer too. I found a new and until now untried cache of ten packs of lamb rogan josh which added to the somewhat limited menu remaining. All the long-life food had begun to taste the same and I often dreamt of fresh food. As the sun went down I enjoyed the new curry flavour, watching the world go by.

A few hours later another severe squall caught me out again, this time with the light spinnaker set. It was pitch black with fork lightning. A gale of wind built in seconds and I rushed to release the guy from the primary winch before we were knocked flat. As the guy ran out I was not quick enough in getting out of the way and, as the wind reached 35 knots, the tail end of the rope whipped off the winch drum, wrapping around my calf with a force that knocked my leg in the air as if I were demonstrating a John Cleese funny walk. I was left with a ten-inch contusion across my calf muscle, opening the skin behind the knee. As I groped forwards and struggled to pull the squeezer line down to save the flailing sail the pain still had not hit me. Even with the sail depowered the squeezer needed to be winched down over the sail as we charged downwind through the blackness. Amazingly, the light spinnaker survived with only minor damage and I got it down and below just as the pain virtually immobilised me. With the video cameras running below I moaned in agony as I pulled on a compression sock, wondering what sort of kinky movies I was making now. Then I dosed myself stupid with strong painkillers and thanked my lucky stars that the injury had not been more severe – I still had my lower leg!

11

Stop – Go to Southampton
(Day 140 – Day 167)

The wind shifted to north-east, indicating that I was now on the northern side of the doldrums belt. It was clear that this was moving very quickly. The Inmarsat confirmed the fact, showing that the belt had moved over 300 miles during one twenty-four hour period, its centre being now at 4° North again, sixty miles to the south of me.

Thunder squalls, known here as West African storms, continued to pass over during the next two days, the record wind change during one of these being a 12-knot tail wind to a 43-knot screaming head wind in just seconds, and twenty minutes later back to normal. With the leg injury, moving around the boat was difficult and painful, but I was now wise to the quick changes and resigned to their unpredictability. I scanned the radar in order to act before other squalls struck. One cloud looked so heavy I reefed the mainsail and squeezed the spinnaker before it arrived, only to end up putting it all back up when nothing materialised. On other occasions, when clouds looked completely harmless, I was left fighting to remove sails in driving rain and lightning.

During the night of day 140 I was sleeping on deck again, chiefly to get earlier warning of squalls. At first light the clouds which had stayed ahead all night drew closer and soon crossed with the associated strong wind and rain beneath them. Fork lightning speared out of the top of a truly mountainous cloud bank and as the rain fell small fish jumped clear of the water around the boat. It was a strange sight and seemed like some sort of warning.

Finally, the calms started in earnest, the seas had flattened out and when the wind died completely it took only a few hours for the sea to take on an oily glassiness. When *Group 4* moved at all I headed directly north in an attempt to reach the north-east trades which lay seductively ahead, just out of reach. A seamless grey overcast settled overhead, the temperature rose even further. Sailing around the world is eighty per cent extreme conditions. One moment you are sailing through the freezing cold and gales of the Southern Ocean and the next you are sweltering in the tropics. Perfect sailing days seem incredibly rare.

The next day was just as gentle with winds from the north-west forcing us in towards the coast of Africa. Almost identical conditions had occurred on the Challenge Race and we had sailed within a few hundred metres of the peninsula of Dakar. We could have hailed the lighthouse keeper. Being alone, I did not relish getting too close. The increase in shipping traffic and proximity to the shore would mean restless nights and slow progress. At every opportunity I worked the boat offshore. On the 12th the wind still had not materialised, sails and decks took on a brick red colour from the thin coating of Sahara sand blown through the high jet streams from Africa. Even the sky was tinted pink. Whales breached and swam fast across *Group 4*'s bows. Later dolphins joined in the display, it was as if they were co-operating in play. Fish continued to leap out of the water around the boat and a shark passed just ahead, his fin lowered like a black flag – 'no swimming' it said. I took little persuading.

During the night fleets of small fishing boats appeared out of the red sand mist with worrying frequency. I slept little as *Group 4* pushed slowly into shoal water around the Bijagos archipelago off Guinea-Bissau. At dawn strong currents pulled dangerously towards the coast and unmarked shoals started to appear on the sounder at a depth of twelve metres. I tacked to the west and backed offshore into clearer, safer waters. A few hours later I passed dozens more tiny fishing boats looking like gondolas or sampans, raised at each end, but more suited to harbour work than fishing thirty miles offshore. Hundreds of dolphins, all swimming and leaping together, came close as we left the shallow water. At last a stronger breeze built, sea water sprinkled the foredeck for the first time for ten days, but everywhere I went wind shifts still pinned me in to the coast. Half the time *Group 4* was making little, even no, progress towards the UK. My average had fallen back again and, wherever I steered, the wind continued to head me. The eastern route up the coast began to look as if it wasn't paying off.

During the night of the 13th April the bioluminescence was exceptionally spectacular, bright enough to light the bottom of the sails with an eerie green glow. Dolphins added to the spectacle, leaving bright snake trails of light criss-crossing under and across our path. But I was by now beginning to become an unappreciative audience. All I wanted was to break free into the north-east trades. I hated watching the boat making no progress down the track towards home. I tacked offshore and stayed on the unfavoured tack towards the Cape Verde Islands during the day on the 14th. It was a desperate attempt to find a more 'backed' wind. By evening a cooler breeze had built and, slowly but surely, the wind began to head me, making the north-going tack more favourable. I kept going west, to be sure of getting clear of the land. The broken spinnaker pole had become a nuisance, blocking the companionway. I was getting better at gybing the remaining pole across the boat and I decided to ditch the tube. After stripping the valuable bits off, I tipped it over the stern, where it upended and sank into four kilometres of water.

On the 15th *Group 4* was still heading offshore. I had tried tacking north several times but each time we were headed. During one of the tacks the yankee sheet caught on a winch handle at the mast. I went forward to clear it, carefully staying to windward, reaching and prodding it from the relative safety of the other side of the mast. Eventually the sheet yanked the handle out of the winch with such speed and force it appeared to vanish into thin air. I waited for its return to earth sheltering beneath the boom but I didn't see it again.

Barrages of flying fish came aboard during the night and at first light I was out clearing the decks of ten fish and two squid, all unfortunately a little far gone to make them appetising enough for a breakfast fry up. As I ate porridge in the cockpit, I watched a trawler turn and follow my course. Several hours later it was still there, never coming close but maintaining a half-mile gap astern. I knew of no reported cases of piracy on the West African coast, but being alone I felt a conspicuous target, bearing in mind the poverty that prevails in so many of the countries on this coast. Unlike many long distance yachts, *Group 4* carried no firearms, but I had evolved a bizarre plan which may have deterred potential boarders. When I needed to sleep, Griselda could be dressed in foulies and stood at the wheel as a decoy. Distress parachute flares would become rocket launchers, orange smoke signals could form a smoke blanket and a sea knife lashed to the boat hook as a pike was ready to repel any diehards that got past that lot. Fortunately for the crew of the trawler, they left my wake and headed back towards the coast before having to face up to unarmed combat with Griselda or my back-up armoury.

The shifting head winds continued for two more days. Huge rollers trundled towards us from the north-west, a depression ahead was producing gale-force winds around the Canaries and, though the rollers had travelled south, the wind had not. With the yacht heeling over again as the wind slowly built, I moved carefully around the deck on my injured leg which was improving but still tended occasionally to give way without warning. Ships passed, but overall it was becoming quieter again as we headed out into the Atlantic. On the 18th the wind shifted towards the west as the depression to the north moved across. It seemed unlikely to hold but, whilst it lasted, it was a real pleasure to be making reasonable miles again. Despite the wind, the boat felt slow. I climbed out to the end of the boom to see if I could tell whether I had picked up something on the rudder or keel, but nothing was visible. There were too many sharks about for me to consider a swim, but I felt convinced something was wrong. Eventually, whatever it was just cleared itself overnight and *Group 4* reached target speeds again.

I was reading the chilling and cautionary tale of yachtsman Donald Crowhurst, a competitor in the *Sunday Times* Golden Globe Race around the world in 1968–69. He had set out with others from the UK but never actually left the Atlantic, sending back false positions showing that he was sailing through the Southern Ocean. When *Group 4* was south of Australia, a British operator at Sydney Radio told me that he had been an operator at Portishead when Crowhurst was on his sham circumnavigation. The operators had all known that something was wrong, the directional radio aerials never pointed toward the positions he was giving out, but they felt there was nothing they could do about it. Finally, he disappeared. When his yacht was found he was missing, having committed suicide for fear of being exposed. His duplicate log revealed a tortured mind. I was glad I had kept this depressing tale until I was well on my way home.

On the 19th it became clear that my track was going to be forced through the Canaries again, so I spoke with Charles Rice at Group 4 HQ to arrange another rendezvous. Neither Group 4 nor I wanted to slow progress down now, the frustrations of the past two weeks would have made further delay intolerable, but *Telegraph* reporter and former Challenge crew member, Michael Calvin, was put on standby with a fast motorboat to rendevous with me as *Group 4* charged between the islands.

I crossed my outgoing track on the 20th (day 150), technically having circled the globe. But there was little sense of achievement, it was just another frustrating day's sailing. The wind had shifted against me again. In order to get through the Canaries I needed to sail in the wrong direction, away from the UK.

In the evening I played classical music to simmer down and struggled to keep going in a fading wind. Eventually, I furled the headsails and slept with the soothing sounds of Pachelbel filtering through the boat, undisturbed by the normal sailing noises. By morning on the 21st I was refreshed and much happier. I sipped a mug of tea, watching the sunrise over a glassy calm sea. Soft cumulus clouds graded from fiery red to a starry black, the sky reflected in the mirror calm was nearly perfect, frustrating but beautiful. Mid-morning a slight southerly breeze filled in and, with the light spinnaker just lifting, *Group 4* began to inch her way forward again. A high pressure had begun building around the Canaries, which I needed to get past quickly if I was to pick up the next system that would give the final push towards the UK.

At first light on the 22nd two cloud banks indicated I was on track to pass directly between Gran Canaria and Tenerife and a few hours later the mountainous shapes of both islands were visible under the clouds either side of the yacht. A motorboat appeared on cue from Gran Canaria, moving into the bright sunshine between the islands. *Group 4* was sailing well under spinnaker, rolling through seas similar in every way to those we had sailed through four and a half months earlier. As the launch pulled alongside shouts went up from the Group 4 staff who had also manned *Craftman's Art* on the south-going rendevous. For the next two hours, still sailing under spinnaker, Mike Calvin and I chatted away between the boats. Mike had an advantage over other journalists who reported on the Group 4 Global Challenge, in that he had crewed aboard *Hofbräu Lager*, one of the leading contenders in the Challenge Race, so he knew exactly what questions to ask and the interview ended up more like a friendly conversation. Once we had finished, I transferred the stills and video film across and we waved our farewells. Just 1,500 miles of familiar Atlantic now lay between my life aboard *Group 4* and return to so-called normality. Had I changed? My conversation with Mike had seemed normal enough, I felt fit and well and looked forward to new challenges. I didn't feel different.

The barometer was rising again, I had not cleared the area quickly enough. The high that was building over the islands astern was trying to reel *Group 4* in. Over the next two days I reached north with the asymmetric spinnaker, but a heavy north-westerly swell, the residue of another gale to the north, killed any speed we built up. Weatherfaxes showed strong south-westerlies moving north just out of reach ahead. A phone call through Portishead to Ceri had me in stitches. She told me of how my mother had politely described Griselda as a medical dummy. I feared there might be a deal of explaining to do when I arrived back. Even Ceri had got the wrong idea about Griselda – she is only a £2.99 Christmas cracker-type girl and would hardly have survived a single assault!

Group 4 slipped forward as the wind faded and a bright full moon lit the smooth sea and long northerly swell. At dawn on the 25th I squeezed the last mileage out of what there was with the light spinnaker, but by mid-morning, even 350 square metres of three-quarter-ounce cloth hung limp and lifeless from the mast. Trying to keep busy is the most difficult thing during a calm. I cleaned, baked, read and wrote up my diary – anything to keep my mind off the lack of progress. I collected weatherfaxes from around the world, but Germany, Bracknell and the USA all gave the same picture. A high pressure and ridge extended across my path up to France. Numerous aborted efforts to get going made a cat's cradle of ropes on deck and

below, four spinnakers and the light genoa clogged the companionway, two awaiting repair.

The following day a gentle 8-knot north-westerly breeze kept *Group
4* moving across a totally flat sea. The barometer steadied and I
watched hourly for signs of a fall in pressure heralding a weather
change. During the afternoon a beautiful four-masted schooner
steamed over the horizon and slowly closed with the yacht. *Star
Ranger*, a 200-foot French sailing passenger ship came to within a
quarter of a mile and stopped engines, whilst loutish passengers hung
over the side taking photos and dropping empty beer cans. Then,
without communicating other than the mumbled shouts of her more
drunken passengers, she steamed off again. I was dumbfounded at the
lack of basic seagoing courtesies of the encounter. I was definitely
closing with civilisation.

Over the next few days the wind increased by 2–3 knots, but this
small improvement was enough to transform *Group 4*'s performance.
In pondlike conditions she built up speed and, if held steadily on
course, could close reach at 8 knots, an impressive figure for a thirty-
eight-ton steel yacht. This was easy sailing and I began enjoying
myself again. The finish was in sight and with time on my hands I was
able to tackle a great deal of maintenance. On deck a programme of
winch servicing transformed them to their original slick action, and
gradually the boat started to look cleaner and feel better maintained.

On 29th April with the corner of Spain lying only 100 miles ahead, I
contacted Charles Rice at Group 4 about the final ETA. Over 600
supporters had watched us leave the Solent, now well over 1,200
people wanted to watch *Group 4* arrive back. This would not be
possible if I were to sail straight for the finish. The most accurate ETA
I could give Charles was during the evening of Monday 2nd May, and
of course that would depend on favourable conditions. The only
solution seemed to be to delay the finish by a few days so that we could
be certain of my coming in at an agreed time. I hated this option and
said as much. Every moment I had been on the boat during the past
five months had been devoted to keeping us moving as well as possible
and establishing a record which would be hard to beat. To hold back
now was really going to hurt. To be fair to them, they understood at
Group 4 and in the end Philip sent a message indicating that the

decision was mine. Group 4 would go along with whatever I chose to do. Frustrated, I tried to sleep before making up my mind. When I woke I went on deck and trimmed the boat for best speed. If I were to slow down, this would be pointless. But how could I abandon the discipline of five months?

I had chosen the Solent as the point to start and finish the Group 4 Global Challenge because that is where Chay had sailed from. But he had also established another precedent by delaying his finish to arrive during the peak of Cowes Week activity. As a result British Steel had received the maximum return for their investment and trust in Chay's ability. I searched for a solution that would satisfy everyone. Though I could not bear to stop racing, I also wanted to give the hundreds of *Group 4* supporters the best chance to see their yacht come in.

Chay's mark had been the Hamble Light. Over the years the size and complexity of single-handed yachts has changed so much that this would be an impractical place to start any future events from. The Group 4 Global Challenge Trophy was conceived as a perpetual one, so there was something to be said for not condemning every future competitor to a Solent start. Then I had my solution. The WSSRC logs round-the-world and transatlantic records from a start and finish line between Lizard Point on the south-west coast of Cornwall and Ushant off the tip of Brittany. The Jules Verne Trophy ran to and from this line. It represents a more international place to start and finish a record attempt. I radioed the organisers at the WSSRC and asked if they would acknowledge a separate record to this line, in addition to the time from the Solent. If they would, I could keep sailing flat out, establishing a clean around the world record first, before slowing down to enable a properly organised finish in the Solent. I would lose a few days to Chay, of course, but with a projected 130-day lead over *British Steel's* time a couple of days would be neither here nor there. What really mattered was that any future challenger would need to beat the Ushant/Lizard line time. It was a solution that I could live with and Group 4, friends and family could all be there to see the yacht come in.

The WSSRC hastily contacted all their committee members around the world and got a unanimous agreement. An observer would be stationed at the Lizard end of the line and would officially record my time over it. They would still attend the Solent finish as well, as technically to beat Chay's record I would need to abide by all the rules until I crossed the line back at the Hamble.

Group 4 wanted to keep the Ushant/Lizard record under wraps, even from family and friends, until just before I was due in the Solent. They felt it was unfair on the supporters, who were coming down to Southampton expecting to see *Group 4* sailing flat out for the Hamble line. I agreed, but in retrospect this was a mistake, for we had underestimated just how closely our progress was being watched, and it made life complicated when admitting where I was to well-wishers and the media. When asked my position during a series of calls on the 30th, I said I was just approaching the Bay of Biscay. In fact a fresh breeze had shoved progress along and my ETA at the Ushant/ Lizard line was now early morning on Monday 2nd May. Frantic messages rushed back and forth to the WSSRC to get an official observer in place on time.

Fog in the western approaches and dozens of ships all heading into and out of the Channel meant the next two days were sleepless. During 1st May, while still shrouded in a thick fog, two swallows settled on the yacht, hopping around the decks, inspecting everything, then, as if approving of what they saw, one went below and fell asleep in the forepeak, whilst the other found more comfortable accommodation in the saloon.

I changed the pilots over. With the risk of collision quite high I wanted to be able to regain control of the wheel instantly. At midday *Group 4* sat becalmed with ships crossing all around. After being accustomed to the space of the open ocean it was frightening how frequently and rapidly ships bore directly down on me. I kept look out with the radar and listened to their engine noises, calling any vessels that got too close on the VHF. The prospect of a collision at this late stage was unthinkable but very real.

As the afternoon wore on a light easterly built, the fog cleared slightly, and we slowly gathered speed. *Group 4* closed with the Ushant/Lizard line at over 9 knots for most of the night and by first light Lizard Point was visible on the radar. The WSSRC observer, Michael Ellison, called on the VHF radio as the land slowly emerged out of the morning mist. With me watching the GPS plotter and him sighting across a transit set up on the headland under the lighthouse we counted down to the finish. I crossed the line at 0635 on 2nd May, 1994, recording a total time around the world from the Ushant/Lizard line of 161 days, 17 hours, 35 minutes and 30 seconds. This would be the time any future challenger would need to beat.*

In many ways this was the real finish for me. I still had six days to go before I would sail into the Solent to meet all my friends and family, but the real challenge was over. It was a strange finish, not the one I had imagined, but a quiet affair. Michael Ellison called on the radio, congratulated me and headed off for a fried breakfast. From my position close to Falmouth I could almost smell that breakfast as I ate a bowl of porridge, the only breakfast food left.

We thought that only a few people knew of *Group 4*'s whereabouts. A Thursday embargo had been placed on the press release which would explain about the Ushant/Lizard line and I expected a quiet few days' sailing in the western approaches before finally entering the Solent. But twenty minutes after crossing the line the mobile phone which had been dormant around the world picked up a signal and rang. I answered it, expecting it to be Group 4 control. Unbelievably, it was a reporter from the *Daily Telegraph* and despite my trying to be cagey about my real whereabouts it was clear he knew where I was. Ridiculous as it seemed, I decided to take cover. For the next few days I found a spot near the Scilly Isles which was relatively quiet and hove to in a near gale. Every morning I would be woken by a gentle drumming noise, followed by an extraordinary loud VROOOOM as an aircraft passed just feet above the mast. My heart leaped out of my body every time, and the first time I called them on the VHF to let them know that I was okay. It was a spotter plane, identifying fishing vessels which infringed the international boundaries. A British trawler, fishing out of Falmouth, called me up, having seen me in the same piece of water for three days running. After explaining that all was well, I found that the skipper was a ex-Group 4 guard from London.

I sailed towards the Solent on Thursday 5th May. With the spinnaker set in a fresh westerly breeze *Group 4* surfed down the

* Though 2nd May was day 162, the record is measured from the noon start on 21st November, 1993.

Channel, and a helicopter buzzed low overhead, filming the final approach. On Friday the wind eased down and another helicopter appeared, this time with Philip hanging precariously from the door waving both arms in total disregard for his personal safety. Finally the day that I had thought about for every single one of the 167 I had been at sea arrived. A heavy mist blocked my view of the Needles at first light. Group 4's Vice-President Loek Malemberg with his yacht *Nordine* and a small crew of supporters, including Ceri, followed alongside. They had stood by all night, allowing me to get some sleep in the busy waters outside the Solent.

The forecast had indicated perfect weather for the final sail up to the Hamble line, but as soon as I started to manoeuvre towards the entrance of the Solent, the wind fell out, and *Group 4* was becalmed with just fourteen miles to go. Support boats filled with people expecting to see us charging up the Solent started to arrive at 6 am. By 8 am I was surrounded by boats but still scarcely moving. The tide had turned and now I was finding it hard to make any progress against the strong outflowing current. A gentle wind built, the light spinnaker filled and we seemed to be making progress again. The phone rang constantly, as Charles revised the ETA.

It was soon clear that I was having real problems. The GPS plotter showed that I was now ferry-gliding sideways or even backwards towards the Shingles bank to the north-west of the entrance. Outside observers saw the boat making fair progress, but the flow of water out of the Solent was stronger. There were just two alternatives. I could get the 135-pound anchor out from below decks, a back-breaking job which would have taken too long, or I could drop the spinnaker and head back out of the Solent entrance and wait for more wind and the tide to turn in my favour – an option I hated. After some quick calculations I saw that if *Group 4* did touch the bank she would not lie right over. It would simply mean a four-hour wait for the tide to turn and lift me into the Solent. I pressed on smiling and waving but knowing that shortly I would be aground in a highly public way. Twenty minutes later, after brief periods of hope when the wind picked up sufficiently for me to make the GPS plot show progress, the keel touched and after a series of bumps *Group 4* touched down on the bank stern first. The strong tides over the bank finished the grounding off, pushing us further on with the grinding noises of shingle passing under the keel. I was hard aground in front of the world's press and thousands of spectators.

It seemed ironic. Neptune was having the last laugh and I could only smile at the ludicrous situation I was in. I went below. Everyone imagined that I was doing something wonderful to get myself off. In reality I put the last lasagna in the oven and made a coffee. I was obviously going to miss the celebration lunch!

I felt terrible for all the people who had come down to see *Group 4* sail triumphantly into Southampton, but there was nothing I could do about it. The wind was just too light. Five hours after we had touched on the bank the yacht lifted clear. It was now late afternoon, the wind was as light as ever. I hoisted spinnaker and just squeezed through the entrance to the Solent at Hurst Point, having gybed in record time to avoid being swept on to a bank on the other side of the deep-water channel. As the sun set on 7th May *Group 4* slowly made her way up the Solent, followed by loyal and cheering supporters. I reached the finish line at Hamble Point, drifting across on the tide in pitch darkness, surrounded by cheering support boats. It was over.

After 167 days, 7 hours, 42 minutes and 54 seconds I had set a new record for sailing around the world 125 days faster than Chay's passage of twenty-two years before.

12

The Pinnacle

As *Group 4* made her way up Southampton Water surrounded by well-wishers the pressures of the day lifted immediately. I had completed what I had set out to do and a wonderful calm feeling of satisfaction settled over me. Hundreds still lined the dock at Ocean Village, despite the late evening arrival, the Hampshire Fire Brigade sounded their sirens and I felt overwhelmed by the support of so many people. *Group 4* sat alongside in the marina surrounded by bright lights and the flashes of cameras. She looked as good as she ever had, a new mainsail cover draped over the boom like a well-deserved winner's sash.

After five months alone I was instantly surrounded by smiling faces and thrust in front of cameras. I answered questions as best I could and greeted as many of the well-wishers as possible. Faces floated in front of me, many I knew, some I did not, but without fail they smiled and made what might have been an overwhelming experience more enjoyable. Philip Sørensen handed me the Group 4 Global Challenge Trophy and, standing at the mast between Philip and Chay, the two individuals who had created the opportunity, I lifted it into the air.

At a celebration dinner at the Royal Southampton Yacht Club, just two hours after my arrival, I listened with a feeling of unreality to people saying kind things about the achievement and complimenting the way the boat looked. I had prepared a speech to try to thank the various people who had made it all possible. In the event, my written notes seemed utterly inadequate. Discarding these, I said a few words, hoping that everyone who had put something into *Group 4*'s success realised just how much I really appreciated each and every contribution.

The yacht is a credit to British workmanship. In the space of two years she had sailed westabout around the world twice. Everyone who had been responsible for her construction, the designer David Thomas, her builders at DML in Plymouth, the Challenge Business, the dozens of people who provided the systems which make such a boat work, should be very proud of what they have created.

After 167 days' sailing I had beat Chay's time by a large margin. But the reasons for the 125-day difference have often been misinterpreted. It is not just a question of improved technology or a larger yacht. These certainly had an effect, but the more important reason is simply to do with modern perceptions of what is possible when sailing a large yacht single-handed. When Chay set out he was doing something that had never been done before. Like the first ascent of Everest, the achievement was everything, the manner secondary. Many experienced seamen had said that what he planned to do was impossible. His only reference point to gauge in what time he could expect to sail around the world non-stop was Robin Knox-Johnston's 313 days eastabout in *Suhaili*.

During the 'seventies it was considered standard practice for single-handers to slow down, heave to or even run under bare poles whenever the wind exceeded gale force. Not to do so would have been perceived as unseamanlike. In the 'nineties single-handing has developed to the point that boats are now driven close to their limit twenty-four hours a day, every day. One needs total confidence in the boat to achieve this. In my case the Challenge Race provided the confidence, as well as giving me a good idea of what I could expect along the route.

Even hardened sailors would find it difficult to believe what these yachts have proved capable of. They have been raced upwind in wind speeds of over 50-knots and through Southern Ocean waves, often for days on end. The stresses and strain on hulls, equipment and crews is phenomenal. I doubt that any other boats have been asked to stand up to so much over such a continuous period as the Challenge yachts. More conventional racing yachts would simply not survive this kind of pounding.

With total confidence in my boat, I felt highly motivated throughout to achieve the best time possible. On several occasions, when things got really bad, I kicked myself into action with the thought of making life tougher for the next person who attempts the record. But it is in the nature of a record to be broken and this one is unlikely to last for as long as Chay's did. I have frequently been asked whether I would do it again. I would not, at least not in exactly the same way. If another person makes the commitment to beat this record, the trophy will rightfully become theirs. For my part, I will seek new challenges.

Loneliness was not really a serious problem for me. A person who is prone to loneliness would never want to undertake such a voyage in the first place. I found I enjoyed the solo passage, far more than I expected to, but sailing with a crew is still infinitely more fun. Without a shared response something is missing from each new experience, even if other sensations are heightened.

I believe I understand just how lucky I have been to be able to live out my dream. But I prefer to view it as a pinnacle of success, rather than an isolated peak. I hope that other challenges, whether more sublime or not, will present themselves in the future. If they do, I will grasp them as quickly as I did this one.

APPENDICES

Appendix One:
The Challenge Fleet 67 ft One-Design Yacht Specification

Appendix Two:
The Group 4 Global Challenge Technical Specifications

Appendix Three:
Food

Appendix Four:
Medical Supplies by Dr Campbell Mackenzie

APPENDIX ONE

The
Challenge Fleet
67 ft One-Design

YACHT SPECIFICATION

Rig	Bermudan Cutter Rig	
LOA	67 ft	20.42 m
LWL	55 ft	17.76 m
Beam	17 ft 3 in	5.26 m
Draught	9 ft 3 in	2.82 m
Top of mast from waterline	85 ft 3 in	25.98 m
Height of mast above deck	79 ft 5 in	24.20 m
Displacement	33 tons	
Ballast keel	12 tons	
Sail area		
(inc 100% foretriangle)	1932 sq ft	179.49 sq m
Main	926 sq ft	86.02 sq m
Genoa	1480 sq ft	137.49 sq m
Spinnaker	3780 sq ft	352.17 sq m
Accommodation		
Berths	14 (6 cabins)*	
Saloon	1	
Galley	1	
Heads	2	
Drying/oilskin room	1	
Chartroom/deckhouse	1	

Engine	
Type	*Mermaid Ford 6 cylinder naturally aspirated diesel*
HP	*120 hp*
Generation	*2 × 110 amp hours alternators (Bat. capacity 800 amp hours)*
Electrics	*24 volt*
Watermaker	*Aquafresh 800ED*
Fuel	*418 gal 1900 lt*
Water	*242 gal 1100 lt*
Instruments	*Autohelm ST-50 Series*
GPS	*Magnavox*
SSB radio	*Skanti 8400S*
VHF	*Skanti 3000*
Radar	*Raytheon R20x*
Mast	*Proctor Masts*
Sails	*Hood*
Winches/deckgear	*Lewmar*
Standing rigging	*Norseman-Gibb Dyform*
Running rigging	*Marina*

Construction	
Hull	*50B Mild Steel*
Deck	*316 Stainless Steel*
Designer	*David Thomas*
Working drawings	*Thanos Condylis (C & S Yacht Designs)*
Builder	*DML Devonport Yachts*

* One doghouse berth was added for the single-handed passage.

APPENDIX TWO

The
Group 4
Global Challenge 1993–94

TECHNICAL SPECIFICATIONS

For the Group 4 Global Challenge a minimum of modification work was carried out to improve what was already a superb design for westabout sailing, and also to make *Group 4* more friendly as a single-handed boat. The modifications from standard Challenge yacht specification included:

1 SAILS
Suppliers: Hoods
          Frederiksen
To reduce effort, friction and chafe – major hazards in single-handed sailing – the wardrobe of sails aboard was amended to include:

- A fully battened loose-footed mainsail with lazy jack system and cheek blocks on reef points. An external track was fitted to the mast with Frederiksen cars.
- A roller furling headsail and staysail.
- A 2.2oz heavy spinnaker in squeezer.
- A $^3/_4$ oz lightweight spinnaker in squeezer.
- A 2.2oz asymetric spinnaker in squeezer.
- A 2.2oz MPG lightweight genoa on its own Seafurl roller forestay.

2 AUTOPILOT
Suppliers: Autohelm/Raytheon
- A dual on-line Autohelm autopilot system was fitted at the mast base and in the main cockpit.
- The twin actuators are hydraulic linear versions to cope with the weight of the helm in all anticipated weather conditions.

3 POWER SYSTEMS
Supplier: Power and Air Systems
- A mini diesel generator was fitted, providing A/C and D/C power supplies, negating the need to run the main engine. This addition allowed considerable fuel saving over the previous usage and enabled the batteries to be charged fully every day, for over 300 days if necessary, with the current fuel capacity of 250 gallons and some ancillary stock.

4 SURVIVAL EQUIPMENT
Suppliers: The Challenge Business
          Henri Lloyd
- A full overhaul of equipment was carried out by the Challenge workforce. A spare Standard 'C' unit was placed on board.
- A full set of survival clothing was donated by Henri Lloyd.

5 STRUCTURAL MODIFICATIONS
- 3 new steel ring frames were incorporated in the forward section of the yacht for additional strengthening.
- A new berth was fitted in the doghouse/navigation station (to give quick, easy access to the cockpit).

6 COMMUNICATIONS
Supplier: BT
- A 24-hour control was established by Group 4. BT race-tracking engineers had round-the-world crew members supporting them.

Suppliers: ● Challenge Business ● Hoods Sailmakers ● Frederiksen ● Autohelm ● Raytheon ● Henri Lloyd ● Lewmar ● Regis Electronics ● Power and Air Systems ● Proctor Sparcare ● BT Communications ● Aquafresh ● Peter Lucas Rigging ● Magnavox.

APPENDIX THREE

Food

MAIN MEALS

Spaghetti Bolognese	12
Beef goulash	16
Chunky steak	14
Curried chicken	21
Chilli con carne	12
Chicken & pasta	10
Lasagne	10
Beef stroganoff	10
Indian turkey korma	12
Chicken tikka masala	15
Sausage casserole	20
Lancashire hot pot	16
Chicken casserole	14
Corned beef	10
Tinned prawns	8
Curry sauce	8

SECONDARY MEALS

Potato sauté egg & bacon	40
Potato sauté onion & bacon	30
Rosti	15
Chinese hot & sour pork	10
Indian lamb rogan josh	10
Baked beans & sausage	20
Baked beans	20
Beans & bacon breakfast	3
Beans & sausage breakfast	3
Chilli con carne	3
Spicy vegetable chilli	3
Sausage casserole	3
Chicken casserole	3
Beef stew & dumplings	3
Lancashire hot pot	3
Asparagus tinned soup	4
Veg lamb & beef broth	4
Cock-a-leekie tinned soup	4

FRESH FOOD

Potatoes	sack	Prime cured ham	2
Onions	sack	Honey cured ham	2
Bacon	1 kilo	Eggs	24
Apples	box	Tomatoes	2 kilo
Fillet Steak	1	Oranges	20

GENERAL PROVISIONS

Tea bags	1200	Glucose sweets	30 packs
Coffee	3 kilos	Apricot jam	8
Chocolate	1 tin	Strawberry	3
Refresh	200 sachets	Black currant	3
Milk	300 litres	Marmalade	3
White sugar	10 kilos	Salt	2
Brown sugar	4 kilo	Black pepper	1
Coffee Mate	3 jars	Vinegar	1
Cuppa Soup	70	Brown sauce	6
Coca Cola	48	Tomato sauce	26
Canned Rio	48	Branston pickle	6
Stella Artois	192	Marmite	2
Cornflakes	14 kilos	Crunchy peanut butter	2
Ready Brek	3 large boxes	Mango chutney	2
Porridge	2 large boxes	Lime pickle	2
Margarine	36 small tubs	Cheese spread	1 jar
Corn cooking oil	3 litres	Parmesan cheese	30 sachets
Olive oil	1 litre	Cheese spread	1 jar
Bread mix	80 kilos	Cheddar cheese	14 kilos
Boasters 5 × 24	11 packs		

Cadbury Choc Fingers	2 packs	Peas	30
Rich Tea Biscuits	40 packs	Runner beans	30
Choc Rich Tea	24 packs	New potatoes	30
Digestive biscuits	24 packs	Broad beans	10
Ginger nuts	24 packs	Butter beans	5
Ginger cake indv	2 packs	Sweet corn	5
Syrup cake indv	2	Tomatoes	10
Choc log indv	3 packs	Ratatouille	10
Jaffa Cake indv	1 pack		
Fruit cake indv	3 packs		
Homewheat biscuit	24 packs	Pears	24
Mars Bars 1 × 48	1	Peaches	24
		Strawberries	24
		Raspberries	24

Boiled rice	60		Mandarins	24
Mash potato	60		Mixed fruit	24
Spaghetti	24		Tinned Cream	72
			Evaporated milk	48
			Custard	24

NON-FOOD ITEMS

Speedo towels	4
J Cloths	4
Dettox	3
Frish toilet cleaner	3
Toilet paper	Box
Kitchen rolls	60
Washing up brushes	2
Fairy Liquid	2
Multi-vitamin pills	7

APPENDIX FOUR

Medical Supplies
by Dr Campbell Mackenzie
(Fleet Medical Officer during
the British Steel Challenge)

Getting the correct medical kit together for a circumnavigation is rather like victualling – it becomes easier and better balanced the more times you have to do it. However, the degree of skill in DIY doctoring that can be applied during ocean crossings is very much limited by the prevailing weather conditions and, of course, it is likely that most serious injuries from falls, galley and rope burns or accidents with spars and ropes under heavy loads, are sustained during high winds and big seas.

It is axiomatic that what is needed in a medical kit is something more than just first aid, as for a solo circumnavigator in the Southern Ocean, it has to provide final aid as well. I felt it was important to provide a good extended medical box for, although one might manage without broaching the majority of the supplies, their mere existence is reassuring.

The early circumnavigators seemed to pay scant attention to their health; Sir Alec Rose barely mentions medical matters in his book, *My Lively Lady*, and though Sir Francis Chichester seemed to be well stocked up it was mainly with herbal and alternative medicines. Aboard *Suhaili* Robin Knox-Johnston carried a fairly basic first-aid kit and at one stage was in danger of having to give up his voyage for the want of some simple antibiotics. He did have masses of stomach powders and kaolin mixture, as his legendary corrosive curries certainly meant that no opening medicines were ever necessary! It is said that he used his syringes and needles for removing air bubbles from his compass, bandages for preventing chafe (*Suhaili*'s) and Vaseline for greasing radio terminals. Chay Blyth has an equally healthy disregard for matters medical and I believe all he required were a few plasters, some aspirin and a tub of Vaseline; it is not clear in what capacity the latter was used.

I knew Mike was fit (I tried to turn a blind eye to his smoking habits) and that all that had troubled him on the Challenge Race had been skin sepsis and salt-water boils from oilskin chafe on the nape of the neck and wrists. So I added some extra antibiotics, but in retrospect perhaps not enough. I also knew Mike was an advanced first-aider from his Fire Service training, and would be able to get medical advice en route via the radio if necessary.

Nevertheless, before his departure we discussed several problem areas, such as infections spreading to wounds, broken long bones, fractured ribs and fingers, burns and also the remote possibility of acute appendicitis. We covered all the commonest complaints and constipation and piles seemed to figure prominently in our discussions. I even instructed him on how to push a large bore hypodermic needle into his bladder through the abdominal wall in the event of acute urinary retention. After that session I felt obliged to buy him a stiff drink and I remember him complaining that medicinal brandy did not seem to feature on the list of medical supplies.

The medicines were boxed in a systematic way into Tupperware containers and the whole fitted neatly into a portable aluminium photographer's box. The kit is based on the single-hander's medical attaché case that had been developed by Dr Jean Yves-Chauve of Rhône Poulenc's Sports Medicine Division for BOC contenders and modified to Mike's specific needs.

As far as medical books were concerned, *The Ship Master's Medical Guide* was a must. I would never sail without a copy. I also slipped in *The National Formulary* for checking up on drugs, their use and side-effects. In addition I had compiled my own *Idiot's Guide to the Medical Kit* which follows.

MEDICATIONS

ANTIBIOTICS FOR INFECTIONS

Erythromycin – respiratory and skin infections
Clarithromycin – as above
Ciprofloxacin – urinary infections and gut infections
Metronidazole – dental abscess and deep seated infections, e.g. suspected appendicitis, combined with ciprofloxacin
Flucloxacillin – skin infections
Co. Trimoxazole – urinary infections and sinusitis

ANALGESICS FOR PAIN

Aspirin
Panadol   – mild pain
Coproxamol – moderate pain
Meptazinol – severe pain
Oruvail capsules – joint and muscle pain
Oruvail gel – to rub on injured area
Indocid spray – as above
Local anaesthetic for injection – Bupivacaine – long acting
Local anaesthetic for injection – Lignocaine – short acting

EYES

Chloramphenicol ointment – infections (do not cover)
Amethocaine drops – pain from foreign body (pad and patch and cover)

EARS

Cerumol – removes wax
Otosporin – infected external ear passage

NOSE

Karvol – inhalation
Sofradex – blocked nose – infected
Ephedrine – blocked nose – non-infected

MOUTH
Lozenges – sore throat
Bonjela – mouth ulcers
Gee's Linctus – cough mixture

STOMACH AND GUT
Gastrocote – indigestion
Motilium – diarrhoea
Imodium – vomiting
Dulcolax – constipation
Glycerine suppositories – complete blockage
Gastrolyte – combat dehydration
Anusol suppositories – piles

ALLERGY
Terfenadine – sunburn; stings
Prednisolone – severe allergy

OINTMENTS ETC
Zovirax – cold sores
E45 – general skin care
Lip salves – chapped lips
Flamazine – burns
Betnovate – rashes – no obvious cause
Emla crem – to numb skin before lancing boil!
Mupirocin – 'up the nose' antibiotic

MISCELLANEOUS
Foot rot, vitamins, proplus, sunblock etc.

As well as the medication the kit included: cotton, crepe and conforming bandages; field dressings, plain and paraffin gauze, non-absorbent dressings, triangular bandages; cotton wool – balls and buds, mediprep, swabs, micro-pore tape, assorted water-proof plasters; arm and leg splints with supporting elastoplast and 'Cas-Aid' strapping; skin closure; steri-strips and dumb-bell sutures; eye pads and patches; scissors, scalpel, forceps, syringes and needles, surgical gloves, foil hypothermia blanket, thermometer, tourniquet and a dental kit.